Creating a Committed Workforce

LPL

CREATING A COMMITTED WORKFORCE

Peter Martin and John Nicholls

Institute of Personnel Management

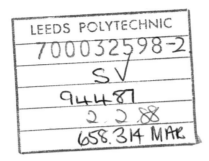

© Institute of Personnel Management 1987

First published 1987

Phototypeset by Papyrus Printers and Stationers Ltd
and printed in Great Britain by
Thetford Press Limited, Thetford, Norfolk

British Library Cataloguing in Publication Data

Martin, Peter
   Creating a committed workforce: the key
   to competitive success.
   1. Employee motivation
   I. Title II. Nicholls, John
   658.3′14   HF5549.5.M63

ISBN 0-85292-379-1

Contents

ROLL CALL OF COMPANIES AND EXECUTIVES

Albright and Wilson Ltd
John Sorrell, Personnel Director, Detergents Division
Bechtel Ltd
Garth Ward, Project Management Co-ordinator
British Steel Corporation
Stephen Best, Director Industrial Relations
Building Design Partnership BDP
Richard Saxon and Bill White, Partners
The Burton Group PLC
Charles Bracken, Group Personnel Director
Bob Falconer, Retail Operations Director, Debenhams
CMG Computer Management Group Ltd
Tudor Francis, Director
Derek Edwards, Director
Barbara Ward, Director
Hardy Spicer Ltd
David Mackin, Managing Director
Jaguar Cars Ltd
Ken Edwards, Personnel Director
Perkin Elmer Ltd
Wally Morgan, Managing Director
John Leane, Business Planning Manager
Pilkington Brothers Plc
Barry Milnes, Manufacturing Manager
Rothmans UK Ltd
Frank Kenaghan, Chief Executive
Paul Neate, Manufacturing Director
Royal Bank of Scotland
Mike Mosson, General Manager, Personnel
Schweppes Ltd
Derek Williams, Managing Director
TI Raleigh Ltd
Derek Hindmarsh, Personnel Director
David Bednall, General Manager, Lightweight

Foreword

This book owes its genesis to a series of conferences on commitment and related subjects we ran in 1983-6 for the British Institute of Management. We listened to a hundred or so speakers from industry and commerce and were struck by what seemed to be a common approach to the creation of employee commitment. Our views were confirmed when we analysed the conference transcripts to pull the diverse experiences together into a coherent picture. From this emerged the 'commitment model' that underlies this book, first published in two articles in *Management Today*. We were subsequently asked by the Institute of Personnel Management to develop our thoughts further, hence this book.

In writing the book, we have had the general reader in mind. Occasionally, there is specific emphasis on the role of the personnel manager, but this is not the main focus. There has been no attempt to make this a formal academic treatment. Indeed, we have deliberately kept the style light and discursive to produce a readable and practically useful book. At the same time, the case studies and the integrating model contain a wealth of valuable material that will be of interest to management specialists, educators and students.

We were spoilt for choice in deciding what to include in the book. Eventually we decided on fourteen case studies, chosen to represent a cross-section of industry and commerce, which illustrated the major points in the commitment model. Peter Martin carried the burden of visiting the companies, in some cases up to four times, conducting extensive interviews with people at all levels.

All the companies who were invited to speak at our conference were initially self-selected. All of them had indicated in one way or another, by public statements or in articles, that they regarded the establishment of commitment in their organization as a high priority. It was to this that they attributed a large measure of their success. Before inviting them to speak, experts on the industry in question were consulted to confirm the management's view. We ourselves also examined their claims with care.

Yet, however plausible such claims are, we cannot be sure of the extent to which the companies we studied were *actually* successful in creating commitment or whether that commitment contributed to their success. All we can say is that the managers in question *reported* that their efforts to create commitment met with a positive response and produced a significant improvement.

Readers must judge for themselves. A glance at the names of the fourteen companies reported on here will, however, confirm two things: that the sample covers a broad range of firms — from Jaguar to Burton, from Pilkington to the Royal Bank of Scotland; and that these firms appear to be successfully tackling the challenge of today's difficult business environment.

In looking at an initially self-selected sample, we have taken a different approach from that of the authors of *In Search of Excellence* and *The Winning Streak*. They first of all established the criteria of success, found which companies in their view were successful and then looked at their management practices.

We came at it from the other direction. Here were companies claiming that a large measure of their success lay in their management of people — and, more particularly, in the creation of commitment in the workforce. We examined what the companies were doing and found a great deal of common ground, permitting us to construct the model. Anyone who, like the companies in our sample, feels that the creation of commitment is important to their success can use this book as a guide. It will give them access to the experience of others, encapsulated in a series of case studies and a unifying model.

We cannot, of course, claim that our research was academically rigorous. Who indeed can do so in a field where the variables for success include not only people within the organization but also complex forces — economic, social and political — without? What did seem remarkable to us, however, was that the commitment model which we developed consistently made sense of the practices of a wide diversity of organizations in remarkably different circumstances. This finding made us feel we had something of value to contribute.

This feeling has been confirmed by the ready acceptance that the

model has had in the training and consulting that we have don
with a variety of companies. Managers at all levels have found tha
the model makes sense and provides useful guidance in developin
their own plans for creating commitment.

We would like to take this opportunity to express our gratitud
to those who, despite the pressures of business, have given so
generously of their time, have spent many hours in discussions witl
us and with great patience have read through several drafts of ou
case studies. Their names appear in the frontispiece which lists the
companies reported on in our sample. Although the companie
concerned made extensive comments on our draft case studies, an
errors are of course our own.

Finally, we would both like to thank Sarah, Jeremy and Michae
and Jane, William and Kate, our wives and children, for putting u
with us as we tried to write a book at the same time as run a busy
consultancy. Their tolerance made our commitment possible.

A note to the reader

This book is based on fourteen case studies of companies that illustrate the creation of commitment in a variety of ways in a variety of businesses. From this experience, an overall unifying model has been evolved of the general processes involved in the creation of commitment (see pages 14–15).

The case studies have been grouped into nine chapters (Chapters 3–11). These nine chapters correspond to the nine facets of the three pillars of commitment in the overall model. Each of these chapters is preceded by a brief introduction to the particular facet of the model in question.

The grouping of the cases has been made for convenience in reading. Naturally, the cases chosen for a particular chapter have some relevance in illustrating the particular facet of commitment being covered. Beyond that they will, more often than not, have relevance to other facets as well. From this viewpoint, the assignment of the cases to particular chapters has been somewhat arbitrary. Many of them could as well have gone 'here' as 'there'. Several of them could have lent support to almost any chapter. Thus, when reading the cases, the reader should not look solely for those aspects which support the particular facet of commitment that is the subject of that chapter.

A quick appreciation of the model can be gained by reading Chapter 2 alone. This is based on the original *Management Today* articles and shows how the case material supports the structure of the model. Understanding can be deepened by reading the introductory sections of Chapters 3–11, where each facet of the commitment model is amplified. Dipping into the cases will then confirm, in more detail, the ways in which commitment can be created.

Chapter 12 surveys US experience in this field and shows how the same concepts and practices are being applied across the Atlantic. It provides an interesting confirmation and counterpoint to the UK experience described in the cases.

In Chapter 13, a look is taken at how commitment might be created in an organization, using the model and case evidence as a guide. It also briefly presents the ideals of 'transforming leadership' that support efforts to create commitment. The final chapter, Chapter 14, puts the recent shift towards recognizing the importance of commitment into perspective and draws some conclusions.

Busy managers might well confine themselves to Chapter 2, for an overview, and then read the case, or cases, which most closely approximate their type of company. Chapter 12, on US experience with commitment, provides a supplement — while Chapter 13 on 'Achieving a Committed Workforce' helps to give some impetus to an action plan.

Managers with more time might then read the introductory sections of Chapters 3–11, which amplify the nine facets of the model, starting with those that are of most interest or concern. This could be backed up by reading more of the cases, as seems appropriate. For a deeper understanding, the introductory and final chapters put the creation of commitment into perspective and draw some conclusions.

Few readers will tackle all the cases, but they contain a wealth of detail on current practice in this area in British business. From this viewpoint, they represent useful case study material for university and college lecturers to build into courses on motivation, leadership and organizational behaviour. They offer an insight into what actually goes on in industry and commerce, as opposed to what the text books say should go on. In the cases, students will see examples of front-line managment practice and will gain some insights into the processes that daily confront managers and managed alike.

1
The importance of commitment

Throughout the developed nations of the world, there is nothing less than a revolution taking place in the way work is organized and managed. In Sweden, Germany and, above all, the USA, company after company is adopting practices that until recently would have been rejected as impracticable, idealistic or downright foolhardy.

People are being trusted. People are being listened to. Work groups are being left to organize their own workloads while management hierarchies are being flattened. Artificial distinctions, both horizontal and vertical, are being removed. Control systems are being simplified, bureaucracies dismantled. Responsibility for action is being pushed downwards and freedom of manoeuvre increased at all levels.

And the result? Productivity surges, while quality rises. Defective output all but disappears, along with absenteeism, turnover and formal grievances. Innovation abounds and change becomes a way of life. It is not unusual for improvements to be by a factor of ten, while doublings and treblings are commonplace.

Do these claims sound exaggerated? The evidence in this book may help to convince you otherwise. Take three examples! Jaguar have increased their productivity by a factor of three from 1.3 cars per worker per year to 3.9. British Steel at Llanwern is making as much steel today as it did five years ago, but with 40% of the work-force. Pilkington, in their new St Helen's plant, have only three levels of management, instead of up to seven, and have abolished overtime, giving time off in lieu, with dramatically reduced absenteeism and non-attendance due to sickness.

There is no doubt that a tremendous reservoir of talent and enthusiasm exists to be tapped in workforces everywhere. A recent Work and Society study reported that 71% of the workers, from a broad sample in the UK, felt uncomfortable when not working to their fullest capacity — even when the work was boring or unimportant. In the same survey, 73% felt that they could be at least 'somewhat' more effective than they are now; and an impressive 17% put it at twice as effective! The Protestant work ethic is still alive and well, in spite of all the stereotypes to the contrary.

The cases presented in this book give many examples of firms which have taken advantage of this potential and benefited from the positive impact of commitment. Chapter 12 presents a summary of similar experiences from the USA, where productivity improvements of 30% to 50% are being obtained — attributable solely to practices which create commitment.

Will British industry be able to join this revolution and reap its benefits? Yes — if it wants to; if it is willing to accept the evidence of others; to react to the examples that are already working here; to absorb the lessons that they bring. No — if it is unwilling to discard the assumptions and attitudes that have stunted its economic development since the Second World War, if it ignores the demands of increasing global interdependence; if it fails to invest in technology and adopt new management practices.

The problem is that too many British managers do not actually believe in the revolution. What proof is there, they demand, that trusting people, involving them — creating commitment and all that — actually leads to higher productivity and better quality than the traditional authoritarian approach? In a scientific sense, very little. But then, how many management decisions are scientifically provable? Management is all about judging probabilities in an uncertain world. If managers waited for certainty before making an investment, launching a new product or attacking a new market, they would soon fall by the competitive wayside.

And yet, until recently, management in the industrialized nations has adopted a cautious and risk-averse attitude towards the use of people. People have been regarded as factors of production with limited capabilities. They work best when the job has been simplified as much as possible, to minimize the chances of error and reduce the need for training. An automatic and standard response was all that was expected. Any improvement in products, process or productivity would come from the application of managerial skill. The workforce would not be expected to contribute to this, but merely to comply, with as little resistance as possible.

As a consequence, workers have felt powerless in their jobs, have found little meaning in them or satisfaction in doing them and have been increasingly isolated in smaller and smaller sub-units. It is as if, in effect, work had been arranged to make it as unsuitable for human beings to perform as possible. Work of this nature satisfies none of the basic human needs.

Research by Professor McLelland at Harvard has indentified three fundamental human needs: for power, achievement and affiliation. Far from recognizing these needs, it seems as if work is often organized to ignore them or frustrate them as much as possible. Workers in their workplace are rendered powerless over their environment; their work is limited and disjointed, giving no sense of achievement; and their isolation prevents satisfaction of the need for affiliation. No wonder, then, that they have been disinclined to show commitment by giving all of themselves while at work.

The phrase 'giving all of yourself while at work' encapsulates what we mean by the word 'commitment' in this book. It entails such things as:

- using all of one's time constructively
- not neglecting details
- making that extra effort
- getting it right first time
- accepting change
- willingness to try something new
- making suggestions
- co-operating with others
- developing one's talents/abilities
- not abusing trust
- being proud of one's abilities
- seeking constant improvement
  enjoying one's job
  giving loyal support where needed.

This is a broad list, but one that is readily comprehensible. A committed workforce is one that is pulling together, with everyone doing their best, and getting satisfaction from the common effort to do as well as possible. People feel they belong, are excited by their jobs and have confidence in management.

A model of how firms are creating commitment – this 'willingness to give all of yourself while at work' – is presented in the next chapter. Meanwhile, let us continue to consider the arguments used to deny the importance of creating commitment.

Apart from insistent demands for proof, another line of defence adopted by the macho management school against evidence of success from the creation of commitment is the 'fallen angel' syndrome. Any firm cited as an example of successful practice is carefully watched for any sign of subsequent trouble. If and when a slip occurs, this is gleefully seized upon as a sign that all is not so rosy after all and that the benefits of participation are illusory, short-lived and exaggerated.

A classic example of this was the famous *Business Week* front-page story with the dramatic headline **Oops!** In it, a half-dozen or so of the forty-three 'excellent' companies in Peters and Waterman's best-selling book *In Search of Excellence* were shown to have suffered difficulties of one sort or another. The clear inference was that the conclusions of the book were somewhat suspect.

The interesting thing, however, is that analysis of the difficulties faced by the firms in trouble was entirely in terms of how they had violated the eight 'principles' of excellence. Far from being disproved, these were, in fact, reinforced by this evidence which showed troubles arising when the principles were *disregarded*.

Be that as it may, one must guard against the 'fallen angel' argument. In the examples in this book, we are not claiming that the efforts to create commitment were solely responsible for whatever success the companies had. Nor, by the same token, should any setbacks that occur be ascribed to failure of commitment. No management is perfect and no company will have unvarying success. Set-backs are *always* possible.

TI Raleigh, for example, was a company in difficulty in many ways, for many reasons (as we discuss in Chapter 8). Nevertheless, the transfer of their lightweight bike operation from Worksop to Nottingham *did* go smoothly and produced results that delighted everyone — workers and management alike. Rothmans have had to shut down some factories for broad economic reasons. This does not invalidate the success that was achieved in creating commitment while the factories were working. Jaguar cars recently had a strike, analysed in Chapter 13, but that does not mean that five years of steady progress have been in vain.

The circumstantial evidence for the value of effectiveness of participation and trust is all around us — and becoming stronger by the day. Take three examples from the cases presented in this book:

Jaguar Cars, in traditional manufacturing; CMG, a leading computer software company; and Perkin Elmer, makers of high-technology scientific instruments.

Jaguar has dramatically improved its productivity and quality. John Egan says this is largely due to their changed approach to people – informing them, giving them a share in success and making them directly responsible for quality themselves. Why doubt him? The computer software firm CMG is growing at 20% p.a. and maintaining high profitability. Tudor Francis, their personnel director, says this is largely because of their open personnel policies and common ownership through the employee share plan. Why doubt him? Wally Morgan, managing director of Perkin Elmer, says their high productivity, reflected in a 20% annual bonus, is closely connected to their value-added, gainsharing scheme. Why doubt him?

In the USA, Rosabeth Moss Kanter, an eminent sociologist, matched 47 companies that took a 'progressive' view in their management of people with 41 taking a more conservative approach. Reporting on her work in *The Change Masters*, she found that the progressive firms were both more profitable and faster-growing.

Of course, there may be other factors involved. Markets may have turned easier, new investment may have been made, exchange rates may have moved favourably. But it is strange to find so many managers from so many companies in such diverse industries all claiming the same thing – all seeing a cause and effect relationship between their efforts to create commitment and the superior results being achieved. Exactly the same is being said in every other developed country.

The encouraging thing is that the three examples above and all the other evidence in this book are from UK firms, often in unglamorous or traditionally depressed industries. The cases and examples we present show what can be done by British managers with a British workforce. This evidence gives the lie to those who say that Japanese success in Britain is not reproducible or is due to special factors that make it irrelevant.

Even without this evidence, however, can one ignore what the Japanese have done and are doing? Time after time they have bought failing UK factories and, in very short order, boosted productivity, while reducing defects to unheard of low levels. While writing this, the newspapers are full of stories of expansion plans of Nissan at their Washington plant in Tyne and Wear. Is their success due only to having a greenfields site, government subsidies and superior products — or whatever other advantage the sceptics advance? Or could it be largely due to their management of people — informing them, involving them, making them feel they belong; giving them excitement in their work by trusting them and making them accountable? Why else would interview after interview with the workers produce the same story? The feeling of release, of uplift, that they express is in stark contrast to what they had experienced in the traditional UK engineering workplace.

A similar success has been achieved in returning Dunlop to profitability since it was taken over two years ago by Sumitomo. This turn around in the performance of typically under-invested factories with truculent, unionized workforces certainly cannot be attributed to uniquely favourable conditions. And yet a transformation has taken place. 'We have been given the investment the company needed and set free to manage things,' a Dunlop production manager is quoted as saying.

This stands in stark contrast to traditional British managers, who are sometimes criticized for their fundamental lack of knowledge of the manufacturing process. According to the Japanese, they are 'defensive, authoritarian, conservative, poor at consultation, protective of their status and hug the chain of command'.

⊕ Convert To Problems ⊕

Fundamental forces

Section 3

The Japanese have thoroughly scared us and opened many people's eyes to what can be done. There is, however, much more to it than that. There are fundamental forces in the business environment that are pushing all companies in the same direction, towards greater reliance on commitment — with a more open style and flatter management hierarchies. Among these are:

(i)   increasing technological complexity
(ii)   the information/communications revolution
(iii) a rapidly growing service sector
(iv)   global competition.

Evidence of the first of these, *increasing technological complexity*, is all around us. Companies in even quite basic industries are constantly being faced with machines and equipment of space-age sophistication. Vastly more efficient and versatile than anything previously seen, such equipment is also more complex to understand and control. Thorough training is required if the equipment is to be usable at anything like its full potential. Maintenance requirements are similarly more demanding.

There is no point in investing in modern equipment to increase one's competitive advantage while doing nothing about recalcitrant unions and untrained, defensive workers who make it impossible to use properly. Not only that, the possibilities that arise, through technology, of integrating related activities are wasted if there is no change in attitudes and practices. Clearly, technology is pushing in the direction of management by commitment.

This is abundantly evident, of course, in the so-called 'high-tech' industries. These are employing an increasing proportion of people who work with their brains. Robert Kelley has christened them 'gold-collar' employees, in his book of that title, in contrast to the traditional blue collar/white collar split. Who can tell if the knowledge-based employee sitting at a desk is daydreaming or wrestling with the complexities of the task? Bright people will always do enough to get by. But is that good enough — what about the wasted opportunities? Such people will only perform up to their potential if they are 'turned-on'; if the working climate gives them that sense of belonging and excitement that makes them feel committed.

The second force, *the information/communications revolution*, is part of the increase in technological complexity, of course. But it is sufficiently special and all-pervasive to be treated separately. The information/communications revolution affects all firms, whether they view themselves as high-tech or not. No one is immune to the competitive threat of rivals who streamline their operations or obtain better access to their customers through the use of information/communications technology.

Furthermore, the incredibly enhanced ability to store, access, process and transmit vast amounts of data very quickly is breaking down barriers. New product development is no longer tied to sequential steps of research, design, engineering and production. Information/communications technology, through CAD/CAM and the associated data bases, makes closer liaison and overlap between these departments not only possible but highly beneficial — both for better products and shorter development lead times.

In offices, insurance companies and banks, the same thing is happening. Departments that were formerly distinct — and very often hostile — entities are being forced by information/communications technology to work together. It is nonsensical, in view of the new capabilities, to maintain the same workflows and relationships as before. Operating the same system, and merely passing the equivalent of pieces of paper from person to person electronically, not only fails to reap the benefit of information/communications technology but, very often, makes things worse.

The formation of teams, drawn from several departments and working together, is necessary to deal with the work flow in an integrated way. These teams can take advantage of vastly increased information-handling capacity and the ability to communicate it effectively to the place where it is needed. Such teams, crossing boundaries and exploiting the technology, will only work well in an open and co-operative climate of commitment. Thus, the general state of technology, and information/communications technology in particular, are pushing in the same direction.

The spread of technology is being paralleled by *a rapidly growing service sector*. More and more people at work are in direct contact with the customer. Not only that, but competitive pressures are making existing firms more conscious of the importance of their employees who are in contact with the public. Most people will have heard of the training that has been done by British Airways, for example, in its 'Putting People First' campaign to improve passenger service.

Such programmes take account of the fact that good customer service can only come from employees who are committed to giving it. It cannot be ordered or forced on them. There are myriad 'moments of truth' in the chain of contact between the customer and company. Management cannot stand behind people every second of the day to check that they are making the most of these moments of truth. Service can only be rendered in an efficient, cheerful and high-quality way by people who feel that the customer is important and are committed to doing their best.

Finally, *global competition* is making us all aware that productivity, quality, creativity and innovation are essential ingredients of survival in today's marketplace. Look at the checklist at the end of this chapter. Sort out those factors that can and cannot be achieved by compulsion. Then consider which of the listed factors are most important for the success of your organization. The changes are that most of these are the very ones that *cannot* be achieved by compulsion!

Competitive levels of productivity and quality cannot be achieved by people who are uninvolved, alienated and dispirited. Creativity and innovation are fatally handicapped in organizations that treat people as automata, half-wits or loafers. The cases and examples in this book show what can be done in the other direction by creating commitment and making people feel that they belong and have some excitement and interest in what they are doing. This, in turn, requires a management style that takes a positive view of people and provides the leadership that creates commitment.

Leadership is, in fact, a key to creating commitment; the sort of leadership that releases energy and makes people feel that they are contributing to a worthwhile enterprise. Such leadership, open and trusting, creates a vision of what the enterprise could be and a climate that enables subordinates to perform to the utmost of their abilities. Called 'transforming' leadership, it is more fully described in Chapter 13.

The challenge for British management

Although the Japanese have scared the rest of the developed world by their success and have shown the way forward in their management of people, the management challenge as we approach the close of the century in fact reflects the more fundamental forces discussed above.

To be successful in the coming decades, managers must respond to these forces and meet the threefold challenge of learning to:

(i) manage people whose output is becoming more difficult directly to monitor or control. These may be technical experts working with their brains or service workers interacting directly with the customer

(ii) manage increasing technological complexity. This means creating the climate in which people will understand and welcome technological developments. In particular, barriers must be overcome and systems changed to take advantage of rapidly developing information/communications capabilities

(iii) manage to achieve significantly higher levels of performance and innovation than hitherto. International competition makes constant demands for higher productivity and quality. These, in turn, demand creativity and an openness to change permitting continuous innovation.

Rising to this management challenge requires, first and foremost, a fundamental psychological shift by most British managers. An implicit feeling is widespread that Britain is doomed to steady and inevitable decline; that we will be forever second best — or worse; and that no amount of effort will bring us out on top.

The first requirement is, then, a belief among managers that their company, division or department can do better; a belief in a different, successful future; and a belief that Britain can change. Without this fundamental belief, deeply and passionately held, the necessary effort of will to effect a change cannot be forthcoming. It is not too strong to say that a new vision of future possibilities is needed; a rejection of despondency; a renewal of faith in the potential of people — both managers and managed — to plan, strive and succeed in being the best.

It is our contention that this new vision cannot be generated by managers entrenched in confrontation and coercion. As the fundamental forces in the business environment make the management challenge ever more pressing, creating commitment will more and more be seen to be an essential part of any response. Many firms have already seen this; some of the evidence is provided in this book. It is to be hoped that their example will be a guide and encouragement to those who have yet to understand the challenge or come to grips with it.

Although it is obvious that we are enthusiastic about the power of commitment, we are not saying that it is a magic wand or that it is easy to implement. Clearly, business success depends on a proper product/market strategy. Unless the basic business objectives are satisfactory, all the commitment in the world will not bring results. The demise of People Express, perhaps the ultimate in the new approach to commitment, vividly brings this home.

On the other hand, firms in business difficulties should not regard the creation of commitment as of secondary importance. It can make all the difference. It is perfectly possible for commitment in an organization to release talents and ideas in an innovative and co-operative wave that corrects deficiencies in strategy and overcomes weaknesses in the basic business parameters.

It is also true that creating commitment will be a problem for many individuals and organizations for reasons of personal psychology or organizational culture. The ways that these factors affect leadership and the creation of commitment are explored in Chapter 13.

With these two caveats in mind, what we say can be summed up in five propositions:

(i)   fundamental forces in the business environment are making a new vision, based on commitment, more and more vital to competitive success

(ii) Japanese industry has grown phenomenally and performed astonishingly well in productivity and quality — partly due to its management of people and ability to create commitment

(iii) in the wake of a few leading firms that have long been 'enlightened', and prompted by the success of the many Japanese operations springing up from coast to coast, management in the USA is rapidly recognizing the importance of a committed workforce

(iv) similarly, many leading firms in the UK have already successfully adopted a wide variety of methods to create commitment. As in the USA, Japanese successes in the UK are becoming more frequent — as shown most recently with Nissan on Tyneside and the recovery of the Dunlop operations taken over by Sumitomo

(v)   in view of the above — i.e. fundamental forces in the business environment and the almost universal trend towards commitment — a very sound and well-reasoned case is required from any UK firm that chooses not to actively pursue the goal of a committed workforce as a vital key to competitive success.

If we stand back for a moment and take a longer-term view, it could be argued that managers in the developed Western world, at the end of the Second World War, ignored two vital, well-documented lessons that the Japanese absorbed, adapted and used to devastating effect.

In the first place, the virtues of participatory management have been recognized in Western management literature since the Hawthorne experiments in the 1930s. Indeed, many impressive improvements in productivity were achieved in America during the Second World War by applying participatory practices. Remarkable expansions of capacity were accomplished, without sacrificing quality, by involving people in the design and conduct of their jobs. Peter Drucker (in *The Concept of the Corporation*, based on the experience of General Motors) recognized this and powerfully argued the case for participation in the late 1940s — anticipating, by some thirty years, many practices now being adopted. In the UK, Eric Trist's work along similar lines, at the Tavistock Institute, was published in the same period.

By the time the Japanese turned to America after the war, seeking management expertise from the West to help rebuild their war-shattered economy, all the evidence for the value of participatory management and the creation of commitment was available. In actual practice, though, the Americans were busy churning out goods to satisfy the post-war consumer boom and paying only lip-service to participation. The Japanese, however, being told it was so important, heard the message in their attentive way and went back home to put it diligently into practice.

Similarly, the modern concept of quality control and the asso-ciated idea of quality circles was introduced to the Japanese by W. Edwards Deming and other lecturers supplied by the American government after the war. The Deming Prize, commemorating this support, is still a sought-after trophy in Japan. Deming preached that quality was central to the purpose of the company and demanded a commitment that began at the very top. He combined statistical control methods with the message that the engineers should be out there on the shop floor, not ensconced in remote offices, and that everyone had something to contribute. These con-cepts were absorbed and put to good use in Japan while being ignored in the West. Ironically, the funds for the Deming Prize come from the royalties from his books, which are best-sellers in Japan!

Having seen what a defeated and despised enemy has achieved in the last 30 years by applying these two vital but neglected lessons, many managers in America are determined not to be caught nap-ping again. They are watching how the Japanese are managing people. They are experimenting, rapidly and boldly, with new methods of organizing and controlling work. Much has been achieved and a great re-thinking is in process.

Let us, in Britain, make sure that we learn all that the Japanese and American experience can teach us. Let us also be sure that the lessons from those firms in Britain that have started down the path, as detailed in this book, are absorbed and built on.

Appendix

1. Some of the aspects of working life listed below can be, to a large extent, obtained by order or compulsion — others cannot. Circle the appropriate word for each:

good time-keeping	can—cannot
standard measurable output	can—cannot
creative effort	can—cannot
observance of rules	can—cannot
no 'foot-dragging'	can—cannot
smart appearance	can—cannot
willing/cheerful co-operation	can—cannot
reasonable overtime	can—cannot
willingness to try something new	can—cannot
compliance with standards	can—cannot
enthusiasm towards customers/clients	can—cannot
high-quality workmanship	can—cannot

2. To the left of the items in the above list, tick up to six items which have the greatest importance for the success of your organization.

3. Circle the appropriate word to complete the following sentence:
'Most of the items ticked above are those which CAN/CANNOT be obtained by order or compulsion.'

Most managers completing this questionnaire find that, by and large, the items ticked (i.e. those that are of the most importance to the success of their organization) are the ones that cannot be obtained by compulsion.

2
Creating commitment*

In the previous chapter, we spoke of a revolution taking place in the management of people. Granting that such a revolution is taking place, what is one going to do about it? What can managers do who want to ensure that their company participates in this revolution and is not left lagging behind?

The answer is to observe what others are doing successfully in this area, abstract the essence from it and apply the lessons to one's own particular circumstances. This book provides a rich set of case examples from successful British practice — what others are doing. To help abstract the lessons so that they can be applied to individual circumstances, this material is structured around a conceptual model shown below. The bulk of the book presents the case material on which the model is based, supplemented by a quick look at comparable experience in the USA. In the final chapters, suggestions are made for applying the model and some general conclusions are drawn.

There is nothing magic or immutable about the model. It is simply a way of pulling a great deal of diverse information together to make it more comprehensible and useful. Otherwise, one is left after reading the cases with a long 'laundry list' of things that were done but with no overall picture to serve as a guide to action.

As the model shows, creating commitment has three major pillars:

Pillar 1   A sense of belonging to the organization
Pillar 2   A sense of excitement in the job
Pillar 3   Confidence in management

*This chapter is based on material first published by the authors in articles on 'How to Manage Commitment' and 'How to Create Commitment' in *Management Today*, November 1984 and April 1985.

Problems??

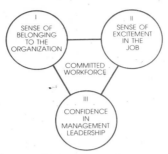

The first pillar is *a sense of belonging* to the organization. This builds the essential loyalty that is necessary to overcome the barriers of 'them and us' that have so marred British industrial relations in the past. A sense of belonging has long been recognized as one of the most powerful forces that binds people together, whether in families, clans, tribes or nations. Managers create this sense of belonging by making sure that the workforce is simultaneously *informed*, *involved* and *sharing in success*.

Giving a worker a sense of belonging is an essential ingredient in gaining commitment. However, being informed, involved and sharing in success will not necessarily be translated into improved results unless the worker can, at the same time, feel *a sense of excitement* about his work — leading to individual motivation to perform. This, second pillar of commitment, can come from an appeal to three higher-level needs: *pride, trust* and *accountability for results*. A trusted worker with pride in his performance will be increasingly willing to accept accountability. In turn, this will reinforce his personal pride and feeling of trustworthiness. This 'virtuous' circle creates a strong individual motivation to perform, with positive effects on commitment and productivity.

Together, the senses of belonging and excitement in the job go a long way towards releasing the talents and energies of the workforce and creating commitment. But they can be frustrated if the workforce does not have respect for and *confidence in management leadership* — the third pillar of commitment.

In recent years, much of British management has gone a long way to restoring its image and regaining credibility. Respect for such management is enhanced by attention to *authority, dedication* and *competence*. The reassertion of authority and renewed dedication to the demands of leadership have gone hand in hand and done much to create a completely new climate. At the same time, more attention is now being paid to fundamentals such as the proper identification of objectives, attention to shop-floor productivity and competitiveness in general.

A sense of belonging

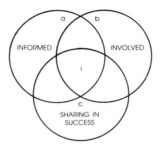

The need to be *informed* is vital in human relationships. Nothing can destroy trust more quickly than a feeling of not knowing what is going on and being cut off from information. The less workers are told about performance and policies, the bigger the possible areas of misunderstanding and the greater the opportunity for deliberate distortion or trouble-making.

Among ways of informing the workforce, team briefing is a structured cascading of information down from top management to the shop-floor. At each level, individuals are regularly briefed by their direct supervisor, so that information is appropriately worded for the listeners. Team briefing is often supplemented by video tapes. When team briefing was first introduced at TI Raleigh, for example, the local managers 'topped and tailed' the managing director's video presentation with an introduction and question session. Similarly, Jaguar Cars puts on a quarterly communications video in working hours in the canteen, with senior directors, including the chairman, present to answer questions. Coupled with team briefing goes an increasing tendency to disclose up-to-date operating information in great detail. In the words of Ken Edwards, the personnel director at Jaguar, 'Information is now being disclosed that a few years ago would have been kept in the boardroom'. Perkin Elmer, makers of scientific instruments, disclose detailed financial information to their staff through the operations of their productivity gain-sharing scheme. Those firms that give broad access to information are convinced that the benefits in increased understanding and commitment far outweigh the possible threats to confidentiality.

If financial information is to have any meaning, it must be presented in a form which can be understood. This means simplifying data and presenting it in a graphical form wherever possible. Albright and Wilson launched a campaign to get worker approval for a new investment project, which would result in increased efficiency, but, also, the redundancy of some 100 workers. The effort took many months and countless repetitive meetings, and was much greater than anticipated; but it was rewarded by the commitment of the workforce to a plan that was initially found unacceptable.

The sense of belonging can be enhanced by making workers feel *involved*, as well as informed. Direct involvement in decision-making is one way, via worker directors or works councils. But probably more important are the 'affective' methods that the Japanese have developed so successfully. For example, there is a strong movement towards single status. Eliminating executive dining-rooms and removing names from reserved parking places — two obvious distinctions — help to overcome the 'them and us' barrier and dramatize the intention of management to involve the workforce.

At a more fundamental level, the traditional distinctions in treatment between shop-floor and staff are being eroded. Clocking-on for manual workers is frequently dropped. Overtime practice is being modified. At a new plant in St Helens, Pilkington found that giving time off in lieu of overtime led to marked reductions in absenteeism and days off sick, as people used such days for shopping, visits to dentists, etc. Perkin Elmer has introduced a single-status pension scheme. Everyone, from the floor sweeper up, gets a pension of two-thirds salary after 40 years' service.

Apart from direct representation, many firms take pains to consult the workforce on investment and organizational changes. This must be done well ahead, giving a real opportunity for the workers' point of view to influence the result. Involving them early on will often complicate decision-making, but the disadvantages are outweighed by increased commitment to the final decisions.

At CMG, a computer software firm, a reorganization plan for its UK and European operations was presented at a very early stage. Despite the uncertainty and discomfort caused, managers concluded that the resulting plan was a considerable improvement on the original, while the involvement of the staff in its evolution produced a high degree of commitment. Similarly, both Pilkington and parts of TI Raleigh gained considerably in commitment from very detailed consultation with their workforces in developing new facilities.

Every opportunity should be taken to create involvement through organized outings, visits and what the Americans call 'hoopla', which UK firms are now markedly more willing to use. They have recognized that inviting the workers' families to visit the factory, for example, can contribute powerfully.

Opportunities often exist to create worker commitment through unrelated events. For example, in 1984 TI Raleigh got workers the same discounts at local shops that had been negotiated for 2,000 dealers coming to Nottingham for a marketing and promotion jamboree. CMG passed on a *Sunday Times* award to enterprising British companies. It paid the difference to take the whisky offered as a prize in the form of 600 miniatures; one was sent to each employee with a covering letter.

Keeping workers informed and involved is unlikely to be very effective if the workforce feels that it is not *sharing the success*. Issue of stock in many smaller, newly created firms is credited with a large role in creating commitment. At CMG, for example, 73% of the stock is now owned by non-founders and 750 out of 1,000 employees owned shares at the end of 1986. Share option schemes are widely recognized as an incentive for top management, and the same principle should apply at all levels within the firm. It does, however, require considerable effort in communications to promote the schemes and made sure they are fully understood. A positive impact is more likely in small companies than large.

Value-added schemes also help to give the employees a share in success. They are based on the observation that in many companies, over long periods, a remarkably constant share of added value is paid to employees in salaries and fringe benefits. This fact is formalized in an agreement automatically to give the workforce the same proportion of any increase in value added as they have received in the past. By this means, attention is concentrated on creating a gain in added value, by improved output or reduced costs, in order to collect the benefits. Perkin Elmer's scheme, introduced in 1978, sharply increased value added over five years, producing annual bonuses of around 10% and now running at about 20%.

Many firms which have not introduced full gain-sharing give lump-sum bonuses. At the Burton Group, no bonus is paid until pre-agreed targets are reached; once the threshold is crossed, a substantial and steeply increasing bonus is payable.

A sense of excitement in the job

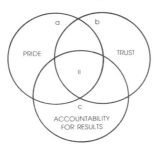

From the earliest craft traditions, personal *pride* has been recognized as one of the well springs of outstanding achievement. One major drawback of modern mass-production is its depersonalization: loss of individual identification with the work. One way of giving back pride is responsibility for quality. Traditionally, companies rely on elaborate quality-control inspection procedures. As with piecework, this is a recipe for confrontation and an open invitation for workers to try to 'beat the system'.

The new approach builds quality into the production process, as the responsibility of the shopfloor workers who do the job. At Hardy Spicer, the quality-control department has been substantially reduced. The number of inspectors was cut from 150 and replaced by 30 quality engineers made responsible to the production foremen. Operators are now directly responsible for the quality of their work. Jaguar has drastically slimmed its inspection department, placing responsibility for quality squarely on the production line. Apart from saving in inspection costs, the quality record has improved substantially. In Edwards's words, 'We now feel that quality is above BMW and very close to Mercedes.'

A related principle is giving people direct identification with their output. When TI Raleigh transferred production of their Carlton prestige bicycles from Worksop to the main Nottingham factory, the move was widely interpreted as meaning the death of quality, so deliberate efforts were made to create a feeling of pride in the work. After six months' intensive training, the workers were certified as 'craftsmen', which was greatly appreciated and valued. Each bicycle in the line carries a tag with a photograph and name of the craftsman who made it, so that workers feel that they are staking their personal reputation on their products.

A sense of competition with rivals can greatly enhance team performance. At the British Steel Corporation's Llanwern plant, productivity is now well up to Western European standards though still behind the Japanese. To bring this comparison to bear on personal motivation, a special communications system enabled employees, from any phone in the works, to get up-to-date figures on output and productivity.

Pride in work can be greatly enhanced by making people feel trusted. Approached in the right way, *trust* brings out people's best efforts to justify the confidence placed in them. Although the principle of payment by results is sound, many companies realize that piecework systems contribute to the adversarial climate and destroy trust. Almost inevitably, the paraphernalia of rate-setting will induce confrontation and a feeling of 'them and us'. Companies as diverse as Pilkington and Jaguar have eliminated piecework and substituted bonus arrangements.

Trust is also developed by reducing direct supervision and transferring more control to the peer group itself; this step has been highly successful at Rothmans' Spennymoor plant. The work flow was organized in parallel group operations, with different activities performed in close proximity by a coherent working group. These groups of workers were given a relatively independent and significant set of activities which cluster together to form a 'whole' task. The pacing of work and the individual assignments were decided by the groups themselves. This successfully eliminated a number of bottlenecks and brought greater understanding of the effects of each activity on the others.

At the new Pilkington glass plant, management left the mechanical craftsmen to decide shift arrangements for routine and emergency work. Removing one management task produced better maintenance performance with fewer breakdowns and emergencies.

Demarcation disputes have long been a feature of British industrial relations. Trust has to become a two-way street to eliminate them. In British Steel plants, trades union co-ordinating committees have been set up. Within these committees, there is a complete integration of the trades unions into a single body for consultations and negotiation. Management directly specifies its requirements for labour flexibility. The committee then undertakes the necessary horse-trading, maintaining union integrity while responding to the competitive pressures of the marketplace. Pilkington's new plant has completely escaped from the tyranny of 'one-man-one-job'. A single category of glass-making operatives is trained in, and willing to use, seven or eight different skills.

Building on personal pride and a feeling of trust, many companies have made workers *responsible for results*. Although some die-hards may resist, it strongly complements other efforts to create trust. Increasingly, companies are pushing decision-making down the line. An enormous amount of practical experience and wisdom exists at all levels. A number of firms now consult shopfloor workers on plant layout and new equipment requisitions well before final decisions are made. Suggestions schemes are taken much more seriously, with efforts made to equal the Japanese suggestion rate: each Toyota worker makes an average of 17 suggestions a year — and over 80% are followed up.

People at all levels can get satisfaction from tasks which are at the limit of their abilities to take them to new levels of achievement. This tendency can be made use of to make jobs more interesting. Of course, stretching people with new tasks is particularly easy in rapidly growing companies, but the same principle has been applied in several traditional firms in mature industries.

Properly used, quality circles can provide the equivalent of the Japanese 'relentless daily quest for productivity improvement', although they cover practically any other aspect of work, too. Williams and Glyn's Bank, before its merger with the Royal Bank of Scotland, had used them successfully to channel the enthusiasm of a young staff into implementing its code of customer service: work flows were improved, seating arrangement corrected, and specific responsibilities assigned.

Confidence in management

In large tracts of British industry, management *authority* had been gradually ceded to shop stewards. A tougher attitude to union power now prevails. At Llanwern, following the four months' strike in 1980, management presented as 'non-negotiable' its plan for a

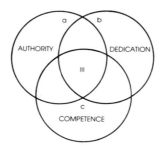

reduced workforce and changed work practices. Far from destroy-
ing commitment, the new attitudes have improved industrial relations. Moderate workers are no longer subject to the whims of more
militant colleagues, and friction is reduced as clarity is restored to
lines of authority.

For a start, managers have begun to distinguish between the
functions of management and the role of shop stewards. There has
been no attempt to undermine them or prevent them from fulfillng
their legitimate functions; but representing members' interests does
not make stewards part of the management team. Managers now
speak directly to their workforce — often through team briefings —
and do not allow stewards to insert themselves in between. Many
firms have also established the principle that candidates for lay-off
will be chosen on grounds of absenteeism, attitude and capability
rather than seniority. BSC at Llanwern and Jaguar are just two firms
which have successfully challenged the traditional last-in-first-out
principle.

It was frequently said that changed management attitudes would
not last at BL once it had been brought 'back from the brink'. But
management's willingness to tighten up was confirmed by the decision to eliminate washing-up time at Cowley. Such discipline is not
a campaign of revenge against the union but is based on the
principle that management *must* function effectively if productivity
and competitiveness are to be maintained.

A competent management team identifies the key factors of success and keeps them constantly before the workforce, with no
compromise accepted in standards of performance in such areas.
Such toughness can be accepted, not as an expression of unexplained
machismo, but as part of a joint campaign to maintain standards and
achieve competitive results.

While reasserting its authority, management has also shown

again its *dedication* to the disciplines of good leadership. Hierarchical levels have been reduced and headquarters' staff drastically slimmed. Management has become more aware of the potential of 'productivity through people'. Management overheads are reduced, sometimes by the removal of an entire hierarchical level, as at Hardy Spicer, where a tier of unnecessary supervision was removed between foremen and managers.

At Pilkington's Greengate factory, an open and trusting style has allowed the management structure to be simplified, with just three levels of management, as against six or seven in the old factory. Similarly, Burton cut the hierarchy from seven tiers to five, while greatly improving performance. ICI's petrochemicals and plastics division shed half its managers.

Although it is not always possible to remove an entire level, much can be done by simply thinning out ranks and increasing the span of control. At Jaguar, for example, the number of production workers controlled by one supervisor has increased significantly. Headquarters staff, too, have been severely pruned in many firms and expensive London offices are closed.

This brings us round in a full circle; one of the major management improvements has been in the principles and techniques, described in this book, for obtaining a committed workforce. Increased willingness to include workers as partners in decision-making and in the rewards of success has made a large contribution to increased worker commitment, which has, in turn, reinforced the open style and started off a new 'virtuous' cycle.

In recent years, management has greatly increased its credibility in many companies by sheer *competence* — by doing a better job. The trigger is sometimes a change of leadership, often a new sense of realism in the face of the recession and the relentless pressure of foreign competition. Management is focusing much more attention on missions and objectives as part of a general improvement in long-range planning and strategy formulation. There is greater awareness of the need to define the firm's distinctive competence and relate this to an increasingly global environment. Correspondingly, managements are held much more responsible for results.

Burton, after failing to recognize what demographic and purchasing power changes were doing to its market, redefined its mission and objectives. It was uncertain whether it was in retailing or bespoke tailoring and, in either case, whether it was in the fashion business or not. These questions were resolved when changed management defined its mission as 'becoming the fashion retail expert of the 1980s', segmenting the market and creating new operations targeted on the segments. This approach revitalized the group and paved the way for its subsequent take-over of Debenhams.

GKN's Hardy Spicer rationalized its objectives by dropping a major unproductive sector, propeller shafts, and concentrating on constant velocity joints. Having redefined objectives, Hardy Spicer took an imaginative management initiative to protect its market. It offered its customers contracts that guaranteed future prices. In other words, it made its customers partners in future productivity improvements, displaying remarkable self-confidence in its own ability to improve performance.

Such initiatives are the second element in improved management. At Schweppes, industrial managers were challenged to reproduce the world's best results in bottling, or come up with specific reasons why they could not. A 'fast-tracker' approach then tested the effects of continuous 100% loading in a given plant. World records have been established in narrowly defined areas, and the improvements were progressively extended throughout the group.

Third, in the great industrial shake-out of the last decade, the tra-high proportion of firms have had a complete renewal of top management. The new professionals are elaborating fresh strategies for remaining competitive in a rapidly changing world. They have become more conscious of the importance of people and the contribution in ideas, energy and enthusiasm that can come from a committed workforce. In the long term, this may be the most important change of all.

Use of the commitment model

The commitment model suggests that the successful management practices which contribute to the creation of a committed workforce can be grouped in three main pillars, each of which has three facets; these are shown, with various examples, in the table and diagram below.

THE PILLARS OF COMMITMENT AND THEIR PRINCIPAL FACETS

Creating commitment **25**

THE PILLARS OF COMMITMENT AND THEIR PRINCIPAL FACETS

Pillar 1 **How to produce a sense of belonging to the organization** ...

... *inform* people by, e.g.
team briefing
open disclosure
simple language and examples

... *involve* people by, e.g.
single status conditions
consultation
outings, visits and jamborees

... *share success* with people by, e.g.
share option schemes
productivity gain-sharing
local lump-sum bonuses.

Pillar 2 **How to produce a sense of excitement in the job** ...

... create *pride* by, e.g.
responsibility for quality
direct identification with output
comparison with competitors

... create *trust* by, e.g.
abolition of piecework
peer-group control
removal of demarcation

... create *accountability for results* by, e.g.
pushing decision-making down the line
challenging assignments
quality circles.

Pillar 3 **How to produce confidence in management leadership** ...

... exert *authority* by, e.g.
no abdication to shop stewards
willingness to discipline
maintenance of standards and objectives

... show *dedication* by, e.g.
reduction of management overheads
seeking productivity through people
attention to commitment

... display *competence* by, e.g.
establishing mission and objectives
new management initiatives
professional standards.

The principal merit of this model is in clarifying the wide variety of managerial practices that contribute to creating commitment. Instead of leafing though a long 'laundry-list' of disconnected practices, a manager wishing to create commitment can use the model as a guide to appropriate action.

The first step would be to consider how a sense of belonging could be created in the organization in question. What could be done to make the employees feel informed, involved or sharing in success? What other actions could be taken to enhance the sense of belonging?

Next, attention would be turned to the sense of excitement in the job. How can workers be given a feeling of pride? To what extent can trust be increased and accountability for results strengthened? How else could the job be made more interesting and exciting?

Finally, attention would be turned to the managers themselves. Are they exercising proper management authority and, at the same time, showing the necessary dedication to their duties? Are they managing professionally by, for example, planning the future strategy of the firm to best advantage and making sure that they have fully analysed their competitive position? Without a fundamental confidence in management competence, efforts to create commitment will almost certainly fail.

A full examination of how commitment can be achieved is presented in Chapter 13. In the meantime, the following chapters, 3 to 11, present the case material on which the model is based.

It is evident from the model — and will soon be noticed in reading the cases — that the various aspects of the three pillars are all interrelated. Most cases contain illustrations of more than one aspect of the model, and some cases contain items from all three pillars — Jaguar cars being a prime example.

It would be an exaggeration to say that every facet of each pillar depends on the others; if one brick is missing, the whole edifice will not fall. It has already been pointed out, however, in the opening of the chapter, that the three pillars themselves are highly interdependent.

A sense of belonging will, by itself, help to create commitment,

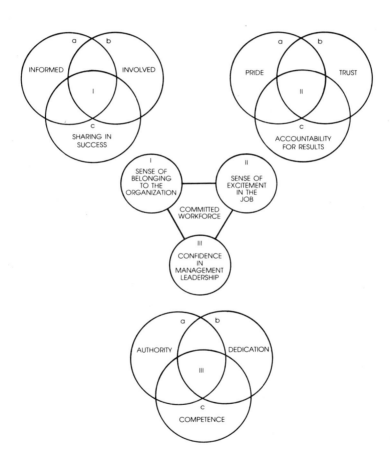

but excitement in the job is needed to inject the necessary enthusiasm to make commitment productive. Yet neither of them will ultimately be effective if there is a basic lack of faith in management competence.

On a more detailed level, it will be evident that involving people in decisions about their work and workplace, in addition to creating a sense of belonging, will also contribute to trust and, thus, help build excitement in the job. Similarly, the abolition of piecework eliminates divisiveness and establishes the conditions in which trust can be created; a sense of belonging can be reinforced by introducing a group or factory-wide bonus to give a share in success.

Management dedication and authority are an essential requirement for the implementation of many other facets of the model. For example, promoting trust by the removal of demarcation boundaries between jobs cannot be done without the necessary determination to confront the unions with the need to change.

Similarly, team briefing is a direct communications link with the workers to keep them informed and make them feel they belong to the organization. This will frequently be seen by the unions as a usurpation of their 'right' to be the only communication channel to the workforce. Management authority must be strong enough to dispute this. Without denying the unions the right to speak to their members, management must firmly insist on their own right to communicate freely, through the chain of command, from the top to the bottom of the organization.

Many other interrelationships will be apparent on reading the cases. These will serve to reinforce the value of the model in clarifying the complexity of management practices needed to create commitment.

3
A sense of belonging: informed

According to Ken Edwards, personnel manager of Jaguar cars, 'Information is now being disclosed that a few years ago would have been kept in the boardroom.' This remark sums up the change that has taken place in British industry and commerce since the late seventies and early eighties. Although practice still varies between the companies we examined, all of them are making far more information available to employees than was the case even five years ago. What is more, the trend is to see how much more information can effectively be disclosed.

Why has this change taken place? What sort of information is being disclosed? How is it being communicated? What obstacles, if any, are there to full disclosure?

First, people need to hear the good news. It assures them that they are working in the right direction and that their efforts are appreciated. Even so, some managers are reluctant to disclose good news. They are afraid that, if they do so, staff will ask for a raise or some other benefit. If, however, staff are told only the bad news, usually coupled with a call for belt-tightening or extra effort, they are likely to take a cynical view of management. The good news, coupled with background information and a foretaste of plans, ensures that employees get the total picture.

In many manufacturing companies, the initial impetus for change arose from the drastic measures taken to ensure that they stayed afloat. The reasons for massive redundancies had to be explained. Above all, the requirements for future survival had to be made plain. Those remaining at work had to be convinced of the reasons for the sacrifices that were being made; they had to understand the pressures of the competitive environment. Without this explanation, it would be difficult for them to accept the need for the increases in productivity and flexibility that were necessary to avoid more cut-backs in the future.

Apart from explaining the crisis and giving the background to changes, there are more fundamental pressures for greater disclosure of information, as touched on in Chapter 1. In much of British industry, the boss is no longer supervising a series of boring and very simple operations in which the thinking power of the operatives is of no consequence. The role of the industrial boss is becoming more akin to that of the boss in a software house. He has to train, explain and be available but essentially let the employee get on with the job. He needs to communicate.

This movement towards more communication is reinforced by social trends. These affect even those who are working in a less technically demanding environment. They may not have the same compelling need to know as their more sophisticated colleagues. They feel, however, that they have a right to know. In the words of one manager we interviewed, 'They may not have been educated at school, but they have certainly been educated by the media. They feel entitled to an explanation.'

What sort of information is being communicated? Obviously, what is being disclosed varies. There does seem to be agreement, however, that all employees show the most interest in matters which affect them directly in their jobs. So, in manufacturing industry, interest is high in matters such as shift output, plant efficiencies, sales through the factory gate and so on. Professional workers, as in architects' practices or engineering construction companies, require either total information about their projects or, at the very least, access to that information.

There seems to be a general view that technical terms such as 'return on net assets employed', 'market share', 'market segment' and 'cash flow', however basic they seem, should be avoided. They are not understood, or at least not appreciated, even by those with a fair degree of management responsibility. Such a lack of understanding is a barrier to communication. Many of the companies in our sample have recognized this barrier and made special efforts to overcome it — by simplifying the language and/or by raising the level of understanding of the employees. Those firms who have taken the trouble to simplify their message and/or to educate their workers report that the investment is very worthwhile.

For example, when Albright and Wilson at their Marchon plant in Cumbria first started to use team-briefing groups to pass on financial information about company performance, they found that their message was not getting across. They had to rethink and try again. The message was simplified several times until the terminology and level of detail became comprehensible.

Perkin Elmer, makers of complex scientific instruments, introduced value added gain-sharing into the company. Gain-sharing, a fairly sophisticated way of sharing value added with the employees, is described more fully in Chapter 5. It can only work if there is the fullest possible disclosure of information. Even with staff as highly educated as those employed by Perkin Elmer, the educational effort in introducing the scheme was significant.

The software house, Computer Management Group (CMG), makes disclosure a way of life. Complete financial information is made available to employees – including everyone's salaries. As one of their new employees remarked, 'I have never known a company so ready to open its books'. Training is provided for those employees who, however talented they might be as computer analysts and programmers, are not versed in the intricacies of finance.

Companies that make the effort to inform their workforces of routine results find they sometimes need to pay particular attention to fuller explanations of the more complex issues. Jaguar, for example, devoted one of their regular video presentations to a thorough and graphic analysis of the competitive strength of the German and Japanese quality car manufacturers

Many organizations operate in particularly complex economic environments and need to communicate even these complexities to the workforce. British Steel, for example, has to wrestle with Community quotas and US protectionism in addition to normal market forces. Unless the workforce, which has already achieved so much, understands what is going on, how can it be persuaded that there is still so much more required?

In the same vein, Albright and Wilson insist on early disclosure of all capital-investment proposals, to gain acceptance of their implications for the workforce. Consultation takes place at the design stage, frequently before the implications are fully appreciated. Although, strictly speaking, the time spent in consultation may seem wasted, useful modifications often result in practice.

Because proposals are presented early, changes in market conditions may cause them to be withdrawn. Although this may be embarrassing, the advantage is that the employees are introduced to the real world of uncertainty that faces management. They see that some management behaviour which they might have thought of as arbitrary is, in fact, a response to changing business conditions. Early disclosure of plans that may be subject to change is, thus, a part of the process of educating the workforce to an understanding of the broader economic and market environment.

Open disclosure of information has added benefits in creating a better atmosphere within the organization. Companies that make a habit of disclosing information on a regular basis comment that there is much less of a problem with rumours. People feel free to ask their manager, or are prepared to wait for an announcement from the company.

Companies also find that, in an environment of disclosure, it is possible to keep confidential any information that really should not be released. The grapevine simply shuts down. People who have access to sensitive information have learned to trust the good faith of management and are prepared, when appropriate, to maintain confidentiality.

We have seen how companies create commitment by disclosing information of all sorts to the fullest possible extent, but how do they go about it?

This varies but since people assimilate information in different ways, there is a case for informing them in as many ways as possible.

One of the most widely used methods for ensuring regular communication is team briefing. Managers and workers are briefed in teams by their own manager or supervisor. They then in turn brief their own teams. By this means information is cascaded down from the board to the shop-floor. At each level, concentration is on matters of local interest, although guided by formal notes provided by the board. These notes are an important feature of team briefing and ensure that everyone in the company receives the same message.

Occasionally there are variations in the levels of management providing the briefing. For example, in Williams and Glyn's, before the merger with the Royal Bank of Scotland, a manager's team was briefed by the manager's manager (the grandfather) in the presence of the manager (the father). This interesting variation has the important advantage of showing top management commitment since the briefing is done by the 'boss's boss'.

Almost universally, when introducing team briefing, companies have found it necessary to train managers in presentation skills. It is common to find that managers and foremen had rarely spoken before to their teams as a group, but always as individuals or in twos or threes.

For the industrial companies in our sample with a poor shop-floor climate, the introduction of team briefing frequently met with indifference or outright hostility. At Jaguar, for example, the shop stewards instructed union members to boycott the briefings. The briefings took place at shift changes and, initially, attendance was low, around 20%. Very quickly, however, word went round that management was being open and presenting very interesting and relevant information at the briefings. Attendance rose within a few months to a very high level and has remained there.

Having the courage and determination to push ahead, against union opposition, with a policy of open disclosure of information requires the exertion of management authority, a facet of the third pillar — confidence in management. This is one example of how the three pillars of commitment are interdependent and mutually reinforcing.

Other aids to communication include videos. Jaguar regularly show videos, every three months or so, and Burton frequently use them. They have an obvious advantage when there are a large number of people to be informed. Company newspapers also have a part to play.

On the spot communication of production information is very useful in maintaining a competitive spirit. In some British Steel plants, for example, it was possible to dial an internal telephone number to find the previous day's production statistics. In some companies, elaborate displays are used to convey results, in others they are chalked up on a blackboard outside the production office.

Striking improvements in communications are reported to have come out of organizational changes, particularly reductions in the levels of management. This is a frequent experience. Pilkington Glass had up to seven levels of management in their older factories. Their new greenfields site opened with three. Their view was that, with too many levels of management, people were under-employed and tempted to do the job just below them, duplicating effort and causing confusion. With fewer levels, nobody has too little to do and everybody knows to whom they report.

CMG has a very simple organizational structure and much MBWA — management by walking about. The structure is very flat. There are a large number of subsidiaries, each with a managing director. Below that, there is only one level of management, the associate directors. Teams are deliberately kept small.

All organizations which move to flatter structures and fewer management levels report significant improvements in communication.

In summary, then, full and open communication is essential for the creation of commitment. People cannot be committed to an organization until they know what is going on. They need to be told the good news as well as the bad. If they are only told the bad, they feel exploited. In today's social climate people expect to be informed. Unless they have information about the organization and its progress and plans, their commitment will be only half-hearted.

Case 1: Jaguar

Jaguar is an example of a phoenix arising from the ashes. It had once been a successful independent company but had been absorbed into British Leyland and appeared to have lost its identity. It had been split up completely. The truck side had been swallowed up by Leyland, as had the bus company. The Daimler and Jaguar manufacturing companies had been split up so that the engine side could be moved into the Leyland engine division, and the assembly side had been put into the BL large-car assembly group. The only part that retained the Jaguar ethos was the engineering department.

When Sir Michael Edwardes was appointed to revive the then bankrupt British Leyland, he decided his best way forward was to unscramble the omelette. Amongst the good things he found a tremendous amount of surviving loyalty to the marques of the various vehicles. People in Jaguar still saw themselves as Jaguar people, as did people in Austin Morris, Rover and so on. To capitalize on this, he decided to break Leyland down again into units with which people could identify. One of these units was Jaguar.

John Egan, a BL man who had left the company in frustration, was recruited as Chairman. His instructions were to recreate Jaguar – a difficult task. Not only did Jaguar have to regain possession of its constituent parts, now buried within Leyland. It had to sort out its financial position from accounts by then absorbed into the total Leyland accounting system. It took nearly six months to determine the level of losses – found to be of the order of £2-3m per month.

Those first months were months of crisis. The company needed to decide who its competitors were; where it should start selling its cars (which by now were selling only through BL); what their new model policy should be; what to do about quality; and how to improve labour productivity.

Labour productivity was 'horrendous'. It took Jaguar twice as long as Mercedes or BMW to build an equivalent saloon – 700 hours as opposed to 350 hours. Since it was going to be impossible in the short run to increase sales to absorb the surplus labour, there clearly had to be major reductions in the workforce. The company was now faced with the familiar problem of having to sack people at the same time as rebuilding commitment amongst those who remained.

Egan felt it was important to take only one bite at the redundancy cherry. The workforce would accept one major cut, but once that had been achieved, those who remained would need to feel secure enough to accept the amount of change that would be required. Forty per cent of the total workforce had to go. On the manual side it was easy to see which jobs were surplus. It was more difficult on the staff side. The company needed to recruit substantially more engineers, so achieving the total cuts required meant that the proportion of staff made redundant had to be even higher.

There were other cost-cutting exercises. For example, canteen subsidies amounted to three-quarters of a million pounds. This could no longer be afforded. At the same time, all the management dining rooms were eliminated. There is now only one self-financing canteen, for employees of every grade, in each of the factories. Incidentally, this is an interesting example of financial pressures hastening a move towards single status.

Another of the cost-cutting moves had profound implications for both management and staff. Investigation showed that something like 11 per cent of the labour force was involved in inspection. Not only was this expensive, but it was found that, on many occasions, actioning the inspectors' recommendations made matters worse. It was decided that many of the inspectors would have to go, and employees would have to be convinced it was their job to build in the quality and to get things right first time.

Getting to that position was, of course, a major operation. First, the company listed all the faults that people complained about. These were divided into three main groups: those which were the fault of the suppliers, those which were the fault of sister companies (for example, Pressed Steel Fisher) and those which were Jaguar's fault.

On the supplier side, the action taken was in principle simple. Companies were told that Jaguar was not satisfied and that business would be taken elsewhere unless new quality standards were achieved. Jaguar would be prepared, at this stage, to allow $1\frac{1}{2}$ per cent of the value of goods supplied as faults. Beyond that, all faults would be paid for by the supplier. After initial difficulties, supplier quality improved dramatically.

Jaguar tackled their own internal quality problems by using task forces. For example, if there was a problem with a steering column, they would set up a group composed of people from all the areas

idea of people
teams of people being able for finding solutions
responsible to problems

A sense of belonging: informed   **37**

likely to have an interest and give them a deadline to solve the problem. No one was appointed especially for the job. People had to do their own job and the task-force job as well. The results of this were, in the words of Ken Edwards, personnel director, 'staggering'. They led to major increases in efficiency and have now become a permanent part of the working scene, providing the mechanism to push accountability for quality down to the shop-floor.

The quality drive was monitored by introducing quality tracking. Every month 100 people in the USA and the UK who had bought Jaguars or their competitors' cars, Mercedes and BMWs, were asked what they thought of the product. Jaguar did rather badly at first, but feel that they are now above BMW and very close to Mercedes, their current target. These efforts to get it right first time and sort out the suppliers are being supplemented by the introduction of statistical quality-control techniques.

As might be expected, all this upheaval caused problems, creating the need for intensive communication with the workforce. This was not happening because Jaguar, in common with so many other companies, was talking only to the shop stewards. Even if they were acting with the best will in the world, which was debatable, shop stewards were inevitably filtering the management message. It became clear to management that their messages were not getting through. To correct this, the Board decided it must take control of the communication process and make communication a major management activity.

The way forward seemed, in principle, to be simple enough. It was to cascade information down from the Boardroom through formal team briefings and to be prepared to use modern aids like video. The questions were, of course, what information? And who should communicate it? 'If', the Board ruminated, 'we want total commitment from our staff, then they should know what they are letting themselves in for'. They therefore decided on complete disclosure: with the exception of some market and competitor-sensitive matters, employees would be entitled to all possible information about the organization. In the words of Ken Edwards, 'Information is now being disclosed that a few years ago would have been kept in the boardroom'.

As to who should communicate it, the answer was, of course, the line managers and supervisors. In practice it was not so simple. The shop stewards argued against briefing meetings and predicted that nobody would bother to attend, but events proved them wrong. At first, in the face of the advice from the stewards to stay away, only a few of the workers attended. It did not help matters that some of the managers and supervisors were found to have no experience of addressing groups and needed to be trained. But in spite of this slow beginning, workers soon realized that management was being open and providing significant information. Gradually the word went round. Now most employees attend because they want to know what is going on.

A chain of communication starts with the monthly board meetings, and information cascades down through the company. Every week, the supervisors have a brief by their factory director on what the factory has done during the previous week, quality achieved and any action that has been taken on domestic issues: housekeeping, toilet facilities and so on. The supervisors use this brief to talk to their teams. In parallel, a management meeting is held monthly outside working hours for managers from the three factories. This provides information on output and plans and includes discussion of the managers' problems.

A communications group, now seven strong, produces a video every quarter dealing with some aspect of the present company position, future plans and so on. People stop work in groups of two hundred or so throughout the factory and come into the canteens and conference centres to see the video. Afterwards, a director is present to answer questions. There is usually a good discussion, though it has to be recognized that not everybody likes standing up at a meeting and asking questions. To cater for this, the directors usually make themselves available at the end of the meeting to answer any individual questions.

Lines of communication were further improved by reducing the layers of management and by trying to make people accountable – using what was, in effect, management by objectives. In organizational terms, everything is made as direct as possible. There is only one person responsible for any given decision. Either it is made in the factory by a designated individual or it is done centrally by someone else. There is nobody at the centre second-guessing people in the factories.

The company was divided into clear operational units. For example, the whole of the limousine side was split off. A manager was appointed and given sink-or-swim profit targets: if he reached them he could stay and if not he would go. In practice, this approach worked well, and each of these separate businesses is flourishing.

Following the major redundancies in 1981, the company was naturally anxious to rebuild a sense of loyalty. The communications meetings had an important part to play, but the directors decided to experiment with family evenings, when the employees would be invited in groups to visit the factories with their families. The stewards were opposed to this and thought the money should be given to the employees as an increase. As the amount involved was only £100,000 – which would mean a derisory increase – the directors decided to go ahead with the idea.

At such an evening there would be an audiovisual presentation showing the families how the cars were made. They would be given a souvenir book about the company depicting all the models made over the years. The evening concluded with a chicken in the basket meal followed by a music hall act. The reception was excellent and, although there were only 7,000 people employed, over 17,000 attended.

Following this success, an open day, the first for about five years, was organized. All the factories were opened one Saturday and the Jaguar and Daimler Drivers' Clubs brought their classic cars and gave a display. This time, 22,000 attended. Gradually, the company image was being restored, along with a sense of identity and purpose.

However, continued recovery depended on even greater quantum leaps in sales, productivity and quality. To maintain and enhance the commitment that had developed, three areas were looked at: the need for skills; further strengthening of communication; and a reward package, including share schemes.

A skilled workforce is essential to a quality car manufacturer like Jaguar. To ensure the development of the necessary skills, Jaguar has adopted an approach to training that can only be described as aggressive. Judging by the positive response to this, the company has tapped an equally strong employee commitment to skills' enhancement.

The most visible commitment to training is the Jaguar Open Learning Scheme. This is no gimmick. Twenty-three per cent of the company's employees are now attending. Its purpose is to provide in-company evening facilities for any employee who wishes to study for a formal qualification, enhance their job-related skills or broaden their knowledge on a wide variety of job-related topics.

The company pays all course and examination fees, but no overtime or reimbursement of travelling expenses.

The courses use lecturers from both inside and outside the company, and, where appropriate, computer-assisted learning which provides individualized instruction at a pace appropriate to the employee. The fifty-two courses range from five weeks to three years and a full listing is given in the appendix.

The most advanced courses include a part-time B.-Eng.-degree and a part-time MBA, at present being taken by ten employees. Two Open University degree courses are offered: a manufacturing programme and one on the industrial application of computers. Both require theoretical and practical sessions using a robot and a microcomputer.

Looking to the future, the company has increased its in-take of apprentices – 250 at present – all of whom are required to be multi-skilled. Overall, each employee receives four days' training a year, at a cost of 2 per cent of turnover. Whatever skills gaps there might be are rapidly and systematically plugged. The training programme is a measure of the dual commitment of the company and the employees to their common future.

To further strengthen communication, Jaguar uses confidential opinion surveys. A recent survey of management and production supervisors was encouraging. It showed there was a high level of commitment to the company and a high level of satisfaction with, and credence given to, communication from above. Output, investment, profitability and quality were all seen to be getting better. The overall level of job satisfaction was fairly high and comparable with other management groups. The level of trust in top management was sound, in comparison with other organizations, though not as high as might have been hoped. A survey of employee opinion gave similar results.

However, there was a very high proportion of managers seeking more involvement than they had at present, and many felt their bosses were not sufficiently 'open'. Nor was there felt to be sufficient opportunity to influence top management or for communicating upwards. It was also suggested there could be better interdepartmental and interfunctional communication. These findings are being used as the basis for renewed efforts to create commitment. As if to show that the path to communication is not easy, Jaguar were hit with a brief strike in October 1986.

Finally, efforts are made to ensure that employees share in

Jaguar's success via section-wide bonuses and an SAYE share-ownership scheme. When the company revival started, all employees were on flat-rate payments. These had been introduced to overcome the problems of the piecework payments system which BL inherited when the company was formed. Piecework pitched one employee against another, and employees against the company. Jaguar now supplement the flat rate with bonuses for both production workers and staff. These are related to productivity and objectives: how much is produced by how many. The staff bonus is half of the manual bonus with the other half depending on how many cars are sold and the number of people employed in selling and engineering.

Basic wages at Jaguar are in the upper quartile for engineering in the West Midlands. Bonuses are a significant part of salary and, together with basic pay, give Jaguar workers the highest wages in the UK motor industry. In addition, there have been three issues of shares; of four hundred pounds in 1984, five hundred in 1985 and six hundred in 1986. At the time of writing, these shares have at least doubled in value. There is also an SAYE scheme taken up by 41 per cent of employees, with high average savings of £31 per month. Finally, a new single-status pension plan has been introduced covering all employees, whether staff or hourly paid.

Jaguar's recovery has been impressive. In 1980, it inherited sales of 14,000 vehicles a year from BL. In 1984, sales were over 33,000 and in 1985, nearly 39,000. In 1980, 40 per cent of the labour force had to be made redundant. As a result of this experience, new job offers are made only where there can be some confidence in long-term security. This means that people frequently work long hours of overtime. Nevertheless, the labour force has increased from an average of about 9,500 in 1984 to about 10,500 in 1985. Of these, just under 300 were engineering and technical staff.

Having set tough objectives for itself, Jaguar is working hard at maintaining and supporting the high level of commitment it has created. The record suggests it is ready for the challenge.

Appendix

Courses available on Open Learning Scheme

seven introductory computer courses (including word processing); three industrial electronics modules; a course on drawing-office practice and one on computer-aided drawing and computer-aided manufacture; courses on computer numerical control; robotics, hydraulics and pneumatics; welding; engineering craft studies; various Institutes' Management Certificates; methods of time measurement and quality control; maths foundation and O and A level courses; English O level; German and French, and English as c second language for immigrants; and shorthand.

Case 2: Albright and Wilson

Marchon, as it is known locally, dominates the town of Whitehaven. Situated on the lonely Cumbrian Coast, North of the Lake District, it is a huge chemical works, occupying 133 acres. The first thing that strikes the visitor, apart from its size, is the apparent absence of people. In fact, excluding 600 white collar workers, there are some 1,200, many working in shifts, scattered about the site – frequently dwarfed by giant buildings, chimneys, pipes and all the complex equipment of a modern chemical plant.

Marchon is the major private employer in the area and whole families work there. Over the years they have seen the site change and grow. It was started as a chemical plant by the partners in a small firm which made firelighters. In 1955 it was taken over by Albright and Wilson, which was itself taken over when Tenneco increased its stake to 100 per cent in the late seventies. Tenneco, a US conglomerate, is a giant by any standards. Its products range from nuclear submarines, through earth-moving equipment via David Brown and nut farming – the company owns thousands of acres of nut groves – to chemicals.

The changes that occurred in the development of the site were considerable and the flexibility required of – and given by – the workforce was impressive. The first chemicals manufactured on the site, in 1943, were components essential for toiletries. Then followed detergent powders.

To reduce dependence on others for input materials, the company decided to manufacture some of its own. One of these was sulphuric acid. An essential ingredient, anhydrous calcium sulphate, just happened to be available in mineable quantities on the site, so the company developed the mine, built the associated kilns and acid plants, and manufactured its own sulphuric acid. It was nothing if not versatile!

So the story continues, with opportunities being exploited as they arose. The company manufactured a wide range of chemicals needed in detergents, and change was part of the accepted order. The operation was profitable, and the long-term forecasts were good. In the late seventies, when Tenneco increased its stake to 100 per cent, Albright and Wilson's turnover was around £500 million.

All that changed in 1980, when in the face of world recession, profits plunged. Tenneco decided to reorganize and slim down to the core business. It was a difficult time and parts of the Albright business were sold off, including flavours, fragrances and fertilizers. Rumour had it that the whole of Albrights was to be sold. That was not true, but maintaining commitment in the face of uncertainty is difficult.

The ownership issue was resolved when Tenneco announced its intention to invest in the site. Albrights was further strengthened by the transfer to its control of additional chemical-manufacturing capacity. The heavy capital-investment programme demonstrated Tenneco's commitment to Albright and Wilson, and turnover subsequently increased.

Management decided that, with the amount of change taking place, there was a need to get accurate information across quickly. It decided to make more use of the briefing groups which had been introduced with the help of the Industrial Society. At the same time, it introduced a tiered consultative council that corresponded to the decision levels in the company.

Communicating with the workforce at Marchon was not completely straightforward. The site produced – and still produces – two different product ranges, detergents and phosphates, each controlled commercially by a different division. The personnel director for the site thus had responsibilities within two different divisions. On the employee side, the blue-collar workers were all effectively organized in a GMBATU closed shop; process workers were in a plethora of up to nine craft unions; staff were predominantly in ASTMS, but some were in AUEW Supervisory and others in TASS. The relationship between the unions was uneasy.

Management's initial objective in team briefing was to put across the financial message, but at their first attempt they fell flat on their faces. The reason was simple. Their message was too complicated. The workforce did not understand the financial terms that were being used, and the first meeting ended in incomprehension. Management retreated and tried again some months later. This time, the message was simplified and understood.

To improve the effectiveness of the briefing groups, management put every one of the 200 foremen and supervisors through a two-day training course – followed a year later by a further day. The courses aimed to improve communications skills and to provide a better understanding of basic financial data. CCTV was used to assist learning.

The climate changed for the better during that first year as

Tenneco moved from divestment to commitment. Lack of profitability became more of a challenge to be overcome than an albatross that would lead to massive job losses. Nevertheless, the warmer atmosphere was soured when management put forward a proposal to rationalize what was called the sulphonation capacity of the plant. This entailed associated job losses of about a hundred, additional to those sustained over the previous few years. The proposal, to invest about £5m, was presented to the Site Consultative Council.

Company policy on capital investment unequivocally states that if there are any implications for the labour force, both employees and stewards shall be consulted. This consultation takes place at the design stage, frequently before all the implications are fully understood. This means proposals can sometimes be introduced and later withdrawn.

In this particular case, the employee view was forthright. They gave the scheme their blessing in principle, but said it must go ahead without any more job losses. Management was equally determined that, for sound marketing and profit reasons, the scheme had to go ahead as planned. An impasse resulted.

Management had the choice to back down or force it through. The latter would almost certainly involve industrial action and, at the end of the day, some compromise on the number of redundancies and compensation. A third choice, which they made, was to try and persuade the workforce that management was right and that the scheme had to be accepted as it stood.

Management embarked on a programme of intensive consultation, with the objective of convincing the workforce on the basis of all the known facts. They called a meeting of the site council at which their basic message was simple. Although the company could sell all the chemicals it could make, manufacturing capacity was insufficient, labour costs were too high and profit too low. Slides demonstrated the sales and profit history of the last few years, and showed forecasts with and without the proposed investment. The final slide showed the manpower reductions required.

Employee reaction was mixed. They were enthusiastic about the good news and devastated by the bad. The shop stewards' committee met and called an overtime ban. Management decided to live with the overtime ban and instituted a series of teach-ins to inform line management about the project. The brief provided was comprehensive and technical.

Management commissioned a beautiful model of all the plant hardware. This was taken round the site and presented to the location councils and the various intra-consultative committees. The model presented a picture of chalk and cheese, of the old and the new, and proved to be very useful. Models are now prepared for all major capital projects.

By this time the unions were behind closed doors and talking about co-operation payments, productivity deals and all the other schemes associated with a heavily unionized environment. Management continued to talk. In the words of divisional personnel director, John Sorrell, 'I do not know how many times these slides were used, but I do assure you that it was certainly more than dozens and probably ran into scores of times. We just kept talking. We talked flexibility; we talked job-release schemes; we talked all the elements we could of softening the blow of this further 100 job losses'.

Management used the briefing groups to do much of the talking. Given the dispersion of employees about the site, that was obviously the best way. It encouraged the foreman and the supervisors to talk to their groups of subordinates about the impact the scheme would have on them. The foreman was, in John Sorrell's words, the 'key to the affair'.

At long last, after months of persistent communication, the craft and general union shop stewards all got together, something unusual on that site. They went behind closed doors for five hours and emerged with a statement saying that they supported the proposal in its entirety. Much relieved, the company used the briefing groups again to communicate the message that the shop stewards had given the proposal their backing and that the project would go ahead unopposed. It was in fact completed, with the associated job losses, in 1984.

The lessons are clear. Management commitment and determination to do the right thing are the key to creating employee commitment. This management commitment spread through every level of management and was all the more remarkable for appearing at a time of great uncertainty. The strength of management feeling meant that employee acceptance was achieved without any false productivity deals, and without improving the scale of redundancy payments. John Sorrell's view was that agreement was achieved by telling the truth. The way forward at Albright was for management to be totally convinced of the proposals' merit and to communicate their message intensively.

4
A sense of belonging: involved

'Home and work — they are two different worlds. At home I am fully involved. There are decisions to make about the children's education and family finances. At work, about nothing. I make more decisions driving to work than I ever do once I get there.' This comment, by an employee in a giant food factory, is eloquent testimony to the frustration felt by many in industry and commerce.

Not all the uninvolved are unhappy. Some claim to be reasonably satisfied. But the evidence from firms trying to create commitment shows a staggering response to opportunities for involvement. Their employees particularly welcome two things — the opportunity both to contribute more of themselves and to gain more control of their working environment; and the opportunity to show family and friends what they do.

In organizations which depend on brain power, involvement is an intrinsic part of the work. People have to be involved in order to do the job. They cannot cope if they 'switch off' for more than short periods. However, even here people are frequently less involved than is desirable. In one service organization we know, work is parcelled out in dribs and drabs and the overall purpose is far from clear. Communication between departments is poor and people feel isolated. They are not advised of decisions and the frustration is palpable.

Organizations with lots of project work, like Bechtel, the giant international contruction group, have an opportunity to involve staff from the proposal stage. At this point the client's intentions, but not the contractor's response, are known. This provides an opportunity for staff to be as involved as they want to be and to contribute as much as they are able. Staff are involved in developing the project plan, an occasion for intense discussion and for people to develop working relationships and commitment. Similar practices apply in the Building Design Partnership, a multidiscipline professional practice in the building industry.

TI Raleigh, in moving production of the up-market light-weight bike from Worksop to their main factory in Nottingham, recruited the workforce from existing employees. Rather than telling the employees how they should produce the bike, management gave them the fullest possible opportunity to contribute to planning and decision-making. The workers were literally shown an empty production area and asked for their suggestions. Management clearly had their own ideas, but there was a significant contribution to the joint management-worker committee from the shopfloor. In spite of predictions to the contrary, the quality bike line was incorporated in the main factory smoothly and with no drop in standards. The workforce developed such pride in the project that they agreed to attach a label to each bike with a photograph of the worker who made it and a note to the effect that the bike had been made to the required quality. Involvement often produces considerable bonuses.

Rothmans have developed a positive approach to employee involvement. It is their belief that there is an enormous reservoir of untapped skill within the workforce. They have attempted to tap this employee resource by using a formal group-working structure to push responsibility and decision-making down the line. Each of the groups performs a relatively independent and significant set of activities which cluster together to form a 'whole' task. The group leaders are trained to seek advice from and utilize the skills of the group.

Pilkington, in setting up their new greenfields flat-glass factory in St Helens, wished to abolish many practices that they felt could no longer be justified. One of these was overtime payments. The compensation agreed was time off in lieu. The absence of the overtime pay structure meant that it became easy to say, for instance, to the six shift mechanical craftsmen that, provided they averaged 39 hours per week over the year, they could arrange the shift patterns to suit themselves. This they are now doing and, in fact, arrange to cover these jobs without referring to the foremen.

The management of change provides considerable scope for involvement. In outline, there are two views about the way change should be handled. One is that changes should be prepared in secret by top management and then announced. The advantages claimed are that this avoids the creation of insecurity and that, although not everybody will necessarily like the changes introduced, at least they know where they stand.

The other view is that the *principles* involved in making the change should be announced, but not the details. The advantage is that, although this creates a great deal of insecurity — questions like 'Who will be my new boss?'; 'What new job will I have?' are bound to be asked — all the relevant issues are brought out into the open and, at the end of the day, there will be a greater understanding of the need for change, a better solution, and greater commitment.

Companies that have tried the second approach have sometimes found it very uncomfortable but have concluded that it is the best way. CMG had a major reorganization in 1984. The Board called in the field managers, explained what was on their mind and told them the details had not been decided. In no time, the phones were ringing and people expressing their concerns. The reorganization took six weeks. At the end of it, the Board met to review their approach. They decided that, although they had at times appeared not to know what was going on, they would approach any future reorganization in a similar way. The benefits of working through the problems and the full consultation involved outweighed the disadvantages.

Such an approach will only work if there is a habit of communication and an atmosphere of trust. If there is no trust and no communication, it is highly likely that change will have to be imposed.

For some local changes or specialist decisions, it is impossible to involve everybody. In such circumstances, companies have found it possible to tackle problems by using working parties, with members drawn from all functions and all levels of the organization. Jaguar, for example, has used such an approach. The members continue with their normal jobs, and the life of the working party is as long as the project. According to Ken Edwards, personnel director, the results of these working parties in terms of improved practices and increased efficiencies were 'staggering'.

Companies have also found that 'open days' and family days are well liked. They help the family put faces to names, see the products and processes and picture the working environment. CMG, after their staff had spent up to four weekends helping to move equipment to new premises following the takeover of part of BARIC, invited the families to look around. The event was a great success.

Jaguar, where at the time there were only 7,000 employees, had 17,000 people attend a social evening at the factories. The format of the evening was an audiovisual presentation showing how the companies made cars, followed by a music hall act and chicken in the basket. Everybody was given a book showing the cars that Jaguar has made over the years. The cost was £100,000 but was judged so worthwhile that they followed up with an open day. The Jaguar and Daimler Drivers' Clubs brought all their classic cars, and 22,000 people attended!

TI Raleigh ran an International Retail Conference in Nottingham. The 2,000 dealers who attended were shown a superb piece of theatre in the form of a marketing presentation. All the employees were invited to the presentation and the accompanying exhibition. The shops in Nottingham were asked to give discounts to the employees as well as the visiting dealers. In the words of the then personnel director, Dick Marshall, 'It created something that was absolutely magic — if you could only get that sense of employee involvement on a permanent basis then you have won the game'. He might have added that such a good feeling could provide a sound foundation for further development. He noted that personnel people should consider the advantages of 'latching on' to the marketing budget, usually so much greater than their own.

Involvement makes an important contribution to the creation of commitment. If staff are not involved and, for example, are not asked to contribute, or if their contributions are ignored, then they are unlikely to have any sense of commitment. To be committed, staff need to feel that their views are valued, and that they themselves can have an effect on the course of events. Involvement does not just happen. Management need to actively create a climate in which the staff want to feel involved. The evidence suggests the effort is worthwhile and the benefits considerable.

Case 3: CMG Computer Management Group

CMG, as the Computer Management Group is known, is a computer bureau and software house. It provides management and computer consultancy to programming services. It also sells accounting systems which it runs on its own main-frame computers, or on the micro-computers that it sells. The market in which it works is booming, and the staff, like many in the industry, are scarce, expensive and professionally aggressive. If they feel their personal technical development is being hindered in some way – for example, by being kept on a particular project for too long – they are likely to complain. If they do not like what CMG is doing, they can easily leave and get a job elsewhere.

In the circumstances, CMG has to pay well, and it has a policy of paying all its staff above the market rate. It does so, not only because it wants to keep its staff but because it wants to employ the best at all levels – from technical and professional through to secretarial and clerical. It is quite happy to describe its approach as elitist. Yet it knows that paying well is not enough. Pay alone might keep the staff on the books, but it will scarcely motivate them to perform, or to be committed.

CMG needs commitment. Operating in a complex environment subject to rapid change, there is simply no way in which the 'bosses' can keep a grip on everything that is happening. There is just too much going on.

Those working for them have to be trained and then trusted to get on with it. If the bosses do not produce a consultant who is trained and committed, then CMG bears the cost of putting faulty work to rights before the client takes delivery. The client must not run the risk of receiving a product of unknown quality subject to the whims of every consultant working on the project. Far from it. The client is entitled to receive a product that works, and that is what he gets.

CMG go out of their way to specify what they mean by 'commitment'. The message put across to those who apply to join is very clear – the commitment must be total. If a job needs to be done, then staff are expected to stay – even if it means working all night. Staff are required to keep a note of their hours of work and this is discussed with them regularly.

CMG, of course, have to give something in return. As well as good pay and opportunities for advancement, they give information, ownership, a share in rewards and an extreme form of single status, probably unique in the UK.

How they share rewards was demonstrated when they won a Sunday Times, J & B Whisky award for enterprising British companies. The prize was 12 bottles of whisky. CMG immediately rang the distillery and said 'Please do not send us 12 bottles of whisky. Send us instead 600 miniatures and we will pay the difference'. The miniatures were given to each member of staff with a covering letter thanking them for the commitment which had contributed to CMG winning the prize.

After its foundation in 1964 with a profit-sharing policy, employee ownership of the company developed slowly and for many years was not heavily promoted. It was always possible to buy shares, but staff were not particularly encouraged to do so. If, when asked, they replied that they would rather buy a suite of furniture, that was the end of the matter.

The impetus for change came in the early eighties, when one of the founder members decided to retire and dispose of his holding of 28% of the shares, valued at just over £1,000,000. The directors considered going to the City or, perhaps, asking their big customers if they would like to buy a part of the organization.

Later, after internal discussions, they realized the full value of staff ownership and went out and sold positively. They stressed the advantages, particularly that of benefiting from the success of the company.

The result was that the shares were oversubscribed and the company had to make an additional issue. At the end of 1986, 750 out of the staff of 1,000 are shareholders and the non-founding shareholding is 73%.

Information is freely available to all staff, even information that most companies would not even consider disclosing. Monthly accounts are made available and, where necessary, staff are trained to read and understand them. Through this approach, staff enjoy the good news along with management and are sometimes concerned at the bad. As an interesting aside, if CMG were publicly quoted, Stock Exchange rules would make it impossible to divulge much of the information currently made available to staff.

In addition to the financial information, CMG is surprisingly free with information about matters such as reorganization. Often, disclosure is made long before management has formulated in detail how the reorganization should take place. Everyone knows the problems that this can create. People can become insecure, worried about their place in the organization, concerned about their promotion opportunities, anxious about who their new boss might be. They can turn their attention away from their job and squander their energies worrying about what will happen to them.

CMG faced such a problem in 1984. The directors decided to reorganize and, in classic CMG manner, called in the field managers to explain what they thought should be done in principle, without going into details. There was, as might be imagined, a lively debate. The managers went back to their subsidiaries and presented the reorganization proposals at the weekly staff meeting. Within minutes, staff were on the phone, voicing their very real concerns about the implications for themselves. The directors were only able to reply that they had not yet reached that level of detail.

The reorganization took a month or so to resolve in detail and put into effect. It was a time of considerable stress. At the end, the managers met to review what had happened. They had been unable to answer their subordinates' initial questions and had given the appearance of complete amateurishness. Next time, there simply had to be a better way. Yet the more they thought about it, the more they realized there probably was no better way. Even without early disclosure there were going to be strains. The directors took the view that the staff were mature and professional and simply had to be treated as such. Overall, the approach had been a success, and they resolved that they would do the same again. A better reorganization plan emerged than the directors had originally thought possible, and there was a high degree of commitment to it since everyone had sweated over the details and developed 'ownership'.

The policy of disclosure is supported by a simple organizational structure and by much MBWA – management by walking about. The structure is very flat. There are a large number of subsidiaries, each with a managing director, and only one level of management below that, the associate directors. These people run very small teams and the manager/subordinate ratio in a subsidiary is about 1:8. Communication is probably helped by the fact that all managers are recruited from within the company.

The Board members are all full-time in principle. For example, even one of the founder members, on retirement, was not permitted to sit as a non-executive director. The Board is active and spends a lot of time with the subsidiaries. There is a programme of two-day visits which are highly organized and include meetings with everyone, including new staff. During these visits, a major effort is made to explain business policies and strategies. The Board has thought about but rejected the use of videos as part of the information-dissemination process. In a relatively small organization it is practicable for directors to speak directly to all the staff, and this is what they prefer to do.

There is also a more formal international structure of senior staff meetings with the Dutch and Germans. Each subsidiary elects one representative per 20 staff or part thereof. These senior staff meetings are hosted by the Board.

Interestingly enough, the Dutch staff were given the opportunity to vote on the introduction of workers' councils. They voted against on the grounds that there was already enough opportunity to discuss policy and strategy at every level of the organization.

Finally, CMG are a single-status organization in a way that must be unique in the UK. All conditions of service are identical and depend only on length of service – except for holidays, which vary with seniority. Certainly there are no separate. canteens for management and staff – that probably would not be practicable anyway in an organization the size of CMG. But there can be few organizations where the directors do not have offices and their furniture is identical to that of the rest off the staff! Nor, perhaps, are there too many companies where the directors have to compete for parking space with the rest of the staff!

Be that as it may, the *pièce de résistance* of single status in CMG is that all personnel files are available for inspection by anybody. The records are simply stored in an open filing cabinet and the office junior has access to the appraisal form of any of the directors. More relevant, perhaps, is that members of peer groups can see what is happening to their colleagues.

The openness and full disclosure practised at CMG does not appeal to everyone. One view is that this approach could work only in an organization made up of aggressive, well-paid and potentially job-mobile professionals. Even then, it probably could not successfully be transplanted elsewhere. However, in 1985, CMG took over the computer bureau part of BARIC and was given a unique opportunity to demonstrate that its culture could take root in a different soil.

BARIC was a subsidiary of ICL and Barclays Bank. It was a bureau, processing other people's data, and also had a networking business. It decided to sell the bureau side, and CMG was the buyer.

BARIC, in the view of some of those who had worked for it, had a different approach from CMG. For a start, it was hierarchical. The managers, in West London anyway, sat in offices on different floors from the staff. Staff were conscious of the differences in status between the various echelons. The payments system was different – there were overtime payments and lots of allowances.

In taking over the BARIC bureau operation, CMG wanted to change BARIC staff to its way of doing things, turning it from an organization with bureaucratic features into one based on complete openness and flexibility. In setting out to so do, it could not have faced a more testing set of circumstances.

It had to deal with a complete intermixing and intermingling, on four of the five mainframe computers, of the bureau and networking sides of BARIC computing. The work was distributed throughout and had to be extracted and separated. Most of the staff, fortunately, were assigned to either networking or bureau business. Although about 10% worked on both, the allocation of staff between the two businesses was relatively easy.

CMG decided to offer an incentive to encourage appropriate BARIC staff to commit themselves before the end of December: the opportunity to purchase CMG shares at the next issue. CMG finally took 150 out of 250 BARIC employees, including five of the junior management.

There was concern amongst some of the longer-serving BARIC staff about the loss of redundancy rights they would suffer on joining CMG. Within CMG they would be given no acquired seniority; the scheme merely met statutory requirements and was not as generous as BARIC's. To that extent, they felt they were taking a risk in joining CMG, though all those who were offered a job joined.

Staff joining CMG received a salary in the CMG mode. This was always a basic with no overtime or allowances. The level of salary offered was discussed first with the BARIC managers who were joining CMG, and the basis of the calculation disclosed. The ICL overtime payments were simply added up and distributed equally.

Those who had done a lot of overtime lost, and those who had done only a little gained. Overall there was a gain, particularly for the majority who had done little overtime and had therefore enjoyed only their basic pay. CMG's general terms and conditions of service were in any case 'bloody good' – to quote a phrase used by one of its new employees; and the entire salary was pensionable and could be taken into account for a mortgage.

Management made a vigorous effort to explain the CMG way of doing things. Managers came in at all hours of the day and night and were prepared to talk to people, individually or in groups. In the early days they took around employees from a previous take-over. Junior management visited other CMG sites and were encouraged to talk to CMG people. They were wined and dined.

The CMG style had an immediate impact on the junior managers who had joined. They lost their titles and offices and had to sit in open-plan offices along with the rest. Most adapted without any trouble and some were quickly promoted. One or two were unhappy at their loss of status.

Most of the staff, too, took to the new style like the proverbial duck to water. They felt reinvigorated. Some felt they were given opportunities that had not been available to them previously. Some reacted against and about 5% left. One or two went back to ICL. Given the abrupt change in culture, the losses were at an 'acceptable' level. Overall, though, CMG management reported there was a lot of goodwill amongst those who were taken over. CMG felt that the takeover was a success and demonstrated that their open style could be acceptable to those from other types of organization.

What really won over hearts and minds was the way CMG set about moving BARIC from ICL's premises to its new offices. There were five moves, in Manchester, Birmingham, Glasgow, Bristol and Feltham (West London). Those outside London took place about mid-year, that in Feltham, by far the biggest site, towards the end of the year. Instead of using removal firms – CMG did not want to face the organizational problems that would cause – it was decided that managers and staff would organize the moves and complete them at weekends.

The UK Services Company move within Feltham took place over four consecutive weekends. Managers and staff came in, unpaid, and physically moved all the equipment, desks and stationery themselves. Directors and managers were there in their shirt sleeves. The company hired vans and had the computers loaded in through the windows by mobile crane. As one member of staff remarked, 'It does you the power of good to see the directors getting stuck in'. And as another put it, 'The move was a first-class example of team-building'. At the end of the move, there was a family day – again at a weekend. Staff were given some time off in lieu, though it is doubtful if all recovered the time they had spent on those weekends.

Now the saga of the move is deeply buried in the firm's culture. It was a major undertaking. As one member of staff said: 'I am really pleased to have done it . . . but, oh dear, I am not sure I would want to have to do it again . . . But perhaps if I have to, I will'.

So, at the end of the day, CMG seemed to have successfully transplanted its culture. A few did not like it, but most people thrived. The openness and ready availability of information seem to strike a chord with staff. CMG's success suggests its policy might well be worth imitating.

Case 4: Bechtel Ltd

Major international construction companies are frequently faced with extraordinary demands on their resources. They regularly meet the challenge of projects worth hundreds of millions of pounds and with very tight deadlines. Some involve employees of up to twenty nationalities from project offices in countries other than their own, using and co-ordinating fabricators on different continents and, in the final phase, meeting and working with representatives from all parties in yet another location.

The challenges posed by these giant projects are immense. They are too complex and too big to be masterminded by a single individual. Each requires teamwork, both to ensure that all interests are fully represented and to generate commitment amongst those who contribute. The actual management of the projects must recognize and reconcile the intense pressures inevitably generated. To meet such requirements, technical and management skills of a very high order are clearly needed. Companies like Bechtel have long faced that challenge.

The Bechtel Group was founded in the USA at the end of the last century and is now a giant. Its roll-call of completed projects includes nearly 300 fossil-fired and 76 nuclear generating plants; 32 hydroelectric plants; over 80 water-treatment and desalting plants; over 100 hotels; 100 oil refineries and over 30,000 miles of petroleum and gas pipelines; plus 40 offshore projects. In the nineteen eighties alone, the projects it has completed are worth approximately seventy billion dollars.

Its British offshoot opened in 1950 and serves as the centre for work in Europe, Africa, the Middle East and the Indian sub-continent. A major part of its work has inevitably been concerned with the evolution of offshore technology for the British and Norwegian North Sea oil fields.

Bechtel has long grappled with the management problems of construction. They know that they must ensure that managers, both on site and at headquarters, understand and respect their appropriate roles; that they must have co-operation and clarity of communications between employees, clients and suppliers; that they need to use matrix management – giving a manager two bosses – but must harness its inherent tensions. They know that, in practice, getting all these factors right is difficult, but that getting any one of them wrong can rapidly destroy commitment, at a cost measured in millions of pounds.

The key task is to build the project team. As a matter of policy, this is started at the beginning – the proposal stage. Staff brought in at this stage are much more likely to feel that they 'own' the project. At this stage the project is won or lost, and the project team knows that they can make the difference between winning or losing. Their efforts are given a useful focus in today's competitive climate, since there is inevitably a client presentation. Preparing for the presentation provides a tremendous welding force and the beginnings of team spirit. On major projects, the company will sometimes facilitate the process by clearing whole floors or areas of office space so that the proposal team can be together.

Once the project is awarded, there are two elements to team building. The first is the straightforward getting together of the team to plan out the job in detail – producing what is known as the thirty-day schedule. That is a stage of intense discussion and argument, giving team members the opportunity to forge working relationships. There is the opportunity to build the same sort of relationship with the client during the regular progress meetings.

The second element comes in the project progress reviews, which are taken very seriously. In addition to the usual monthly reports, a senior management review of every project is held at quarterly intervals or at appropriate 'milestones'. These reviews are very thorough and include a complete reforecast. The company is highly committed to completing projects on time.

In addition, the company uses formal team-building exercises. Many take place in an artificial environment, off-site and away from head office. They are used to bridge some of the gaps caused by lack of self-awareness and knowledge on the part of individuals. In such sessions, Bechtel use training specialists as facilitators, just to make sure, in the words of project manager Garth Ward, that 'things don't get out of hand'. The team-building exercises are time-consuming and expensive, but where they were used, the company believe, they led to major schedule improvements and saved large sums of money.

For example, in one major UK site where work started in 1981, the company spent two days off-site with the construction manager and those reporting directly to him. They looked at what was in it for each of the individuals. What were their personal goals? What was the project about and what were the key milestones? A series of exercises allowed individuals to become more familiar with each others' values. For this the company used a classic leadership game, the Lego brick tower, with an element of competition. Bechtel also tries to involve the client at an early stage in order to build up project relationships for joint success and to remove any win/lose competition between the two project teams.

This particular site had an overriding local issue, which was the power and influence of the trades union officials versus the first-line supervision i.e. the foremen. To redress the balance, the approach was to build up the relationships between the foremen and the next level of supervision, the superintendents and the field engineers. The engineering and supervision groups had been in the company for some time but had not actually worked together.

The programme was a mixture of straightforward training with team-building. Topics covered included industrial relations, safety standards and assertiveness, culminating in a one-day role play reconstructing a case at an industrial tribunal. Finally, the group was asked to contribute to a plan for training the foremen and participated in the resulting four-day programme.

Half-way through the project, time was devoted to a two-day exercise reviewing success and failure. Although, in total, there was clearly a lot of time spent off-site and in training, this was more than compensated for by a saving in construction time of seven weeks (out of seventy) and in money – to the client – of £250,000 (out of £8,000,000) field labour costs.

In addition to its project-based team work, Bechtel takes steps to maintain and enhance its already high internal standards of team work. For example, following a major reorganization, the directors decided that formal team-building exercises would help them work more quickly and effectively into the new organization. They went away for a weekend and, using a proprietary 'preference inventory' as a framework, they worked in pairs to establish mutual expectations. They also took part in the classic NASA moon-survival team-building exercise, with a video recording of their approach used as a basis for a team critique. The directors have also 'critiqued' some of their subsequent real-life internal meetings.

The company uses video all over the world to help enhance organizational team-building. Its approach is somewhat unusual. The President or Chairman will hold a staff forum, and the video of the proceedings will be made available throughout the company. This is the most practical way for top management to communicate with staff scattered over seven continents. Top management, as far as possible, also relies on the principle of 'management by walking about'.

Good team-building helps harness the tensions generated by matrix management. These tensions arise from the conflicting pressures inherent in a tightly run project: the need to get things done, on time and within budget, and the need to maintain standards in areas so complex that they require the attention of specialists.

Organizationally, the conflict is expressed by giving each manager two bosses. One is the project boss whose job, in simple terms, is to get things done; the other is the functional boss (for example, the civil or mechanical engineering boss) whose job, again in simple terms, is to maintain professional standards of work. The potential for conflict arises out of the fact that managers report to a functional senior manager of the same profession. However, when they work within a project team, they report as well to the project boss.

Integration of the functional teams can be helped if it is understood throughout the organization that the project manager will share in the responsibility for performance evaluation of his team. As Garth Ward explains, 'There is no better way to influence an individual's productivity than for him to realize that there is somebody looking over his shoulder at his performance on a day-to-day basis . . . and that that person can influence his pay, promotion, job rotation and training'. In other words, the project manager's assessment of the contribution made by members of his team must be seen to play an important part in their career progression, even though they may not work for him again.

This applies even at the highest levels. For example, on-site there is a construction manager reporting to a project manager whose overall responsibility is for engineering, procurement, construction, commissioning and so on. However, the construction manager identifies his long-term boss as the senior construction manager, usually located at Head Office.

The situation has been described as one in which the constitutional monarch (the project manager) has all the executive power in theory but is not able to exercise it; and the prime minister (the site construction manager) has the direct application of the real power. It is not a happy combination on a construction site. Consequently, to avoid potential difficulties, the site manager is integrated into the home-office team as early as possible in the formative stages of the project.

Matrix tensions also arise in the relationship between the home-office design group and site management. These arise from lack of awareness that the plant is not actually about the design on the drawing board, but about how the design is built in the field. It is the site construction people who have the crucial input into the planning exercise. If they are not integrated into the design team, the potential for conflict is immense.

Team-building has an important part to play, but difficulties can be minimized by a good field manager who has the ability to solve problems in the field. Conversely, those abilities are always going to be required, but good team-building can do much to ensure they do not need to be continuously used.

The amount of management freedom actually enjoyed by the construction company depends on the type of contract agreed with the client. With a lump-sum contract (i.e., the client pays a given sum of money for which he should receive a completed project at the time agreed), the contractor should have complete freedom to manage things his way. The contractor does, of course, have an incentive to save money through innovation, and the client will never completely abandon his interest in day-to-day progress. But, overall, the contractor should have a fair amount of freedom. He has control of his team.

On a reimbursable contract (i.e., the client pays the contractor for costs incurred), the client has a greater interest in becoming involved in day-to-day management. There is a potential for conflict between contractor and client. Establishing common goals becomes that much more difficult, and good relations between the contracting parties are that much more essential.

What contractors frequently prefer is a bonus-sharing scheme between client and contractor, where the contractor enhances his profit by beating mutually agreed goals on, say, schedule completion, fabrication progress and success with team-building.

In spite of all the efforts made to ensure that client and contractor are on the same wavelength, there are still clients who constantly change their minds. This is very demotivating for the project personnel. They can end up not knowing whether they are coming or going, and it takes tough management to maintain their commitment and interest. Constant attention to team-building helps people through this difficulty.

The hallmark of the international construction industry is its sheer scale and complexity. The co-ordination and completion to time of some of the bigger projects seems nothing short of miraculous. Of course, the companies use the most sophisticated planning aids available. They are heavy users of computers for both design and control. They can bring enormous resources to bear. At the end of the day, however, the success of their work depends on the commitment of all those involved. It requires each person to understand both their own contribution and the contribution others make to the overall effort.

Projects can sink or swim depending on people's commitment to the team effort. Bechtel makes time for people; it makes a conscious effort to develop team commitment. This continuous effort is one of the driving forces behind their success.

5
A sense of belonging: sharing in success

How people are rewarded can help create or destroy their commitment. It can determine whether or not they co-operate with the organization, or work only for themselves. It can decide whether or not they put in that extra effort or just coast along. Getting reward right is important.

There are a few basic principles. To create commitment, reward should unite the team and not divide it. It should give people a stake in the success of the organization. It should encourage involvement in the purpose of the organization. The incentive element of reward should be worthwhile and self-financing. The benefits side of reward should be available on the same terms to all who work in the organization. Basic pay should recognize the realities of the marketplace.

Reward should unite the team: any bonuses should be related to the achievement of the organization, or a significant part of the organization, rather than to the achievement of individuals. Within industry there has been a major change in practice within the last ten years. In the post-war period, right up to the mid-seventies, large sections of manufacturing industry, particularly the engineering industries, used individual incentive schemes. Workers were paid a basic rate and a rate for each unit of output they personally achieved. They had no incentive to co-operate with each other and did not do so. Sometimes managers found it impossible to manage: they were told by the workers that the decisions they wished to take would interfere with earnings and were therefore unacceptable.

There were other problems. Workers hoarded production so as to minimize fluctuations in earnings. They found that constant repetition of a job enabled them to beat the calculations of the time and motion people. Incentive targets were thus easily achieved and, in fact, provided no incentive — merely higher pay for less effort. Now more and more companies introduce schemes that encourage teamwork. Most of them reward the employees for two things — for performance in matters over which they have direct control and for performance in matters over which their control is *indirect*.

Pilkington, for example, at their greenfields factory at St Helens introduced a scheme whereby bonuses are paid for factory-wide achievements in efficiency and sales. Efficiency is to a considerable extent directly under the employees' control. Sales are not controlled from the factory except to the extent that employee flexibility and quality contribute to sales results. Employees are thus, broadly speaking, being rewarded specifically on their own team effort in improving efficiency, and on the company's success in selling the product.

The Perkin Elmer value-added scheme is also based on the results of the total organization. Bonus can be earned for improvements in direct controllable costs, excluding labour, and for better sales performance in terms of either volume or price. Again, most employees can only contribute indirectly to sales, but they are encouraged to think in terms of the total organization.

The Burton Group scheme is likewise overtly team-based. Even if the individuals achieve their targets, their division has to exceed its challenging profit target before individual performance bonuses are paid. Hardy Spicer too have a factory-wide bonus scheme (they still maintain the old individual scheme as well, but it is becoming less and less significant).

In all these organizations people have an incentive to work with each other and not against each other. An important part of their reward is based on the performance of the organization of which they are a part. Their incentive is to work with management to achieve improved organizational results, rather than to oppose it on the grounds that what management requires might conflict with their desire for earnings in their individual incentive scheme. People need to be given a stake in the success of the organization. The most popular approach is through the employee share schemes currently available. Oddly enough, this method, despite the tax concessions, seems to be rather more difficult than expected. Companies which offer various types of employee share schemes find that the take-up is low unless they make a positive effort to market the schemes to employees. The Royal Bank of Scotland had a scheme with very low take-up. They brought in consultants to advise them how to sell it internally. The consultants devised a full presentation, which was made initially by them but subsequently by line management. Take-up rose to fifty-five per cent. There are now seven thousand or so employees saving an average of thirty pounds per month.

CMG, although not publicly quoted, has always had an employee share-purchase scheme, but it was never sold very hard and take-up was low. It was only when one of the founder members wished to retire in the early eighties and realize his shares that the directors appreciated the full value of staff ownership; they therefore went to the staff and sold positively. The resulting issue was oversubscribed and now over eighty per cent of employees are shareholders, with the non-founding shareholding at seventy-three per cent.

Reward should encourage involvement in the purpose of the organization. This requires clarity on the part of management as to what the organization should be achieving and on the part of employees as to where they should direct their effort. Clarity is expressed through the mission statement. The targets derived from it need to focus attention on the current business needs and should be more than extrapolations of past trends. They only engage the employees' effort if they are challenging. The Burton approach of having two-tier targets — a fail-safe target which is reasonably easy to realize and another plan that is really challenging (with out-of-the-ordinary rewards for achievement) — has served that organization well.

Likewise, no matter how hard the employees work, if the organization, for whatever reason, does not achieve its purpose, they should not receive a bonus. This is recognized, for example, in the Pilkington bonus scheme, which states that 'management discretion will not be exercised in the operation of the scheme, even if payments are adversely affected by circumstances outside the employees' control'. Employees are thus subject to all the vagaries that affect the company in the real world. Fortunately, the market for glass is such that both parties have found the scheme beneficial, and the employees' real efforts have not been offset by poor market conditions or too many acts of God. This linking of reward to the economic success of the firm, both negative and positive, helps people realize that they are 'all in one boat together'. The scheme has proved rewarding and appears to be popular.

The incentive element of reward should be worthwhile and self-financing, but the difficulty comes in deciding what level of bonus payment, however derived, is appropriate. Ralph Halpern of Burton has no doubts. He believes that the more favourable climate, and particularly the reduction in the top rate of income tax to sixty per cent, has helped to make money matter again and to motivate managers to perform. Bonus levels in his company are high as a percentage of salary, particularly at senior level, and can double an already competitive salary.

The situation at Burton seems to be exceptional. Most of the companies surveyed, and some others not directly reported, seem to operate with bonuses from ten per cent upwards. The Perkin Elmer scheme is currently providing around twenty per cent of base salary. In some companies, manual workers are taking home bonuses of thirty per cent.

Interestingly enough, the alternative of just paying a higher base salary does not seem to be regarded with much favour. Neither the danger of a high bonus — that it will not be paid when times are bad — nor the uncertainty involved in a share scheme receive much attention. The position seems to be that management likes the flexibility provided by bonus schemes, and that workers like the challenge. Paying and receiving some form of bonus, however it is described, is regarded by the majority as an important part of the business of creating commitment.

It goes without saying that bonuses should be self-financing. This ensures that the bonus will only be awarded for activities which bring financial benefit to the organization. It also ensures that management and workers are pulling in the same direction. If bonuses create a net cost to the organization, the management incentive is to stop them being earned.

The benefits side of reward should be available on equal terms to all who work in the organization. People are quite happy for those with more responsibility to be rewarded with more pay — perhaps even with a company car. It is equally true that many people in the present social climate feel that the differences should stop there. They take the view that the distinction between blue- and white-collar worker, between the monthly and the hourly paid, is outmoded.

The consequences of this belief are far-reaching. If workers want staff status, then they have to be prepared to give up overtime. They usually have to be prepared to be paid on a monthly as opposed to a weekly basis. In return, they can expect to belong to the same pension scheme (with benefits dependent on pay and length of service but on nothing else), to receive the same sickness allowances, and so on.

Such developments are already happening. Pilkington has abolished overtime at its greenfields site and at some of the older sites as well. Employees are given time off in lieu. In return, they receive higher earnings. Jaguar has introduced a pension scheme to cover all employees. Albright and Wilson is making progress towards harmonization of conditions of employment for all employees in the UK. The white-collar organizations like Building Design Partnership and CMG already have full equality of terms and conditions with, of course, increased pay for increased responsibility. The trend towards harmonization accords with the spirit of the times, and is a feature of the committed organization.

Finally, pay should recognize the realities of the market-place. Bonus schemes need to be additional to a market-determined rate of pay. They should not be used to bring low pay up to the market rate.

Case 5: Perkin Elmer

Perkin Elmer is a company whose expansion led to a deterioration in industrial relations which needed to be reversed.

The company, an autonomous subsidiary of an American multinational, is a manufacturer of high-technology scientific instruments. It operates in a market that is expanding and competitive, but profitable for those with the right products. It currently employs 874 people in the UK and in 1985 made £6.1m profit on a net turnover of £35.5m.

This UK subsidiary was set up in the fifties in the pleasant residential town of Beaconsfield. Its business prospered, but in 1968 it was unable to obtain local planning permission, and expansion had to take place elsewhere. The company was directed to the development areas and chose South Wales, mainly because it would be easily accessible along the new M4 motorway.

The industrial tradition in South Wales is, of course, quite sharply different from that of Buckinghamshire and the clash of cultures was a contributory factor in the deterioration in industrial relations. Llantrisant, right from the start, had gone the union route. There, in 1968, the AUEW had been granted recognition before the factory had even been opened. Beaconsfield had operated without a union.

However, with growth in numbers, some staff at Beaconsfield began to feel that the atmosphere of the small company was disappearing and that nothing was being put in its place. There was also a feeling that management was more responsive to the union at Llantrisant than to the non-unionized staff at Beaconsfield. In 1975, this led to a request at Beaconsfield for a staff association. Management was slow to respond and, shortly after, an ASTMS branch was established. ASTMS and the staff association co-existed – they still do – and both were recognized in the course of that year.

The net result was a deterioration in industrial relations between the company and its employees; it was even worse between employees, mainly because the unions did not co-operate with each other. Naturally, efficiency in the company declined. The situation continued to be unsatisfactory for a number of years and, in the recession of 1974-5, was a direct contributor to some thirty redundancies. Things could not continue as they were and in 1975 the company started the long climb back to creating a committed workforce.

How they went about it is interesting, because there was no game plan. At the end of the day, the company's real salvation was found in productivity gain-sharing, but that was not known then. At the time, the first step was an attempt to improve communications. The Managing Director, Wally Morgan, started by establishing a weekly operations group meeting with all his divisional managers for R & D, manufacturing, sales and finance – to discuss current events. He made it mandatory for the divisional managers to meet with their departmental managers the next day and for these departmental managers to meet with their supervisors within a week. The quality of the meeting was heavily dependent on the individuals concerned, and some did it better than others, but at the very least it was a step in the right direction.

In 1976 the process was taken a stage further with the introduction of quarterly reviews of the company's operations. These were attended by the whole of the operations group, including all managers, supervisors and union representatives. The Commercial Director gave the presentation, which included full details of orders, shipments, backlog, costs, profits, capital purchases, inventory turnovers and receivables. This was all done in graphical form and as simply as possible. The question sessions were lively and, as a matter of policy, there was the fullest possible disclosure of information.

In 1977, the Board made a commitment to move as quickly as possible to single-status for all employees. The company abandoned clocking-on for manual workers and went straight over from a 40-hour week to a 37.5-hour week. It introduced overtime for all except the Managing Director. (Research and Development staff had to be an exception to this, since they worked flexitime.) The point of this move was not only to treat everybody equally but to provide some compensation for managers who were suffering from the government incomes policy: if they were earning more than £8,500 p.a. they could not be given a salary increase.

1978 was the year for contracting in or out of the state pension scheme. Perkin Elmer decided to contract in but also to have a single pension scheme to which all employees would belong, giving a two-thirds pension after 40 years' service. All members of staff, including directors, belonged to this scheme, and benefits were related only to salary.

Still on the theme of single status, the company moved away

from fixed rates for the job, applicable to manual workers only, to banded rates for all. This meant that all employees were paid on an incremental scale, on which there were 6-8 points to a band, receiving one increment every year until they reached the top of the band. In 1980, some of the tension was taken out of annual wage negotiations with the introduction of index-linking to the Retail Price Index. The company was, of course, fortunate enough to be able to afford such increases. In 1981, all employees were given BUPA cover.

The real breakthrough, the company believes, was the introduction of an added-value gain-sharing scheme in 1978. The scheme arose out of the company's search for some method of motivating and rewarding employees for increasing efficiency. It was introduced to the scheme by Frank Jones, who was an ex-director of Mullards and a Vice-President of the Institute of Electrical Engineers. It was his belief that it was important to measure the added value of a company and to monitor the percentage of that added value which was paid out in remuneration to the workforce. Practical guidance on the introduction of the scheme was given by Douglas Bentley of Bentley Associates.

Added-value schemes are simple in concept, though in practice their introduction requires care. There are two components: sales and the direct controllable costs excluding labour. Added value is simply sales less those costs.

In practice, of course, sales has to be defined more carefully as net sales after deducting commission and adding production for inventory. Direct controllable costs include such items as materials, scrap, protective clothing, journals and publications, tools, energy, maintenance, travel and so on. What remains is added value, which includes wages, salaries, overtime, holiday pay, sick pay and so on, as well as retained earnings, tax and returns to capital in the form of interest, dividends and so on.

The interesting thing is that, in practice, most companies tend to pay out an approximately constant percentage of their added value in remuneration. Perkin Elmer were surprised that this was so in their case, but investigation over a six-year period showed it was. The company paid out a constant proportion of added value in each of its four business sectors – 48%, 22%, 50% and 27% respectively.

The overall employee share of added value for all business sectors was 47.9 per cent. Bentley suggested that the way to establish a scheme was for the company to guarantee to pay the workforce a constant 47.9 per cent of added value as it grew. This would give a direct incentive to the employees to increase efficiency, knowing that 47.9 per cent of any increase in added value would go directly into their pockets via wages or bonuses.

This is all simple enough in principle, but there were in fact two major hurdles to be overcome. The first concerned education. There had to be a major educational effort to ensure that the workforce really understood the scheme, and the benefits to them and to the company.

The second was that the board had to understand that the scheme required the fullest possible disclosure of information, which was not expected to be a problem, and that capital investment had to be made where employee suggestion schemes showed this to be appropriate. In Wally Morgan's words, if the employee suggestion would lead to an increase in added value, 'management would be almost morally required to make that capital investment'.

On the educational side, there was much for both sides to understand and digest. The first was to explore ways in which both management and employees could actually increase the company's added value. There were three basic approaches: the sales value of the products could be increased by selling more or raising prices; external expenditure on component costs and controllable expenses could be reduced; or increases in the salary bill could be limited by avoiding unnecessary recruitment (major savings can be made by employees finding more efficient ways of working). As current bonuses are running at around 20 per cent of basic earnings, it is clear that the possibilities have been fully realized.

To make the scheme fair, employees should only receive a share in the value-added bonus for the times at which they are actually working. Eligible pay is thus defined as basic pay for employees qualified to participate, less any pay that is received while absent: for example, sick pay. It was agreed, however, that bonus would be paid on holiday pay. All employees could participate after three months' employment with the company.

Payments are made quarterly in arrears. The first calculation is of the employees' 47.9 per cent share of added value. The amount available is then determined by subtraction of the pay that has been already distributed in the form of wages and salaries and so on. Seventy-five per cent of this difference is distributed immediately and the remaining twenty-five per cent is transferred to a reserve account for settlement at the end of the financial year. At that point, any surplus in the reserve is distributed and any deficit is absorbed by company. A fresh reserve account is opened for the new financial year.

Finally, company policy is to review pay (maintained in the upper quartile of earnings for the industry) regularly in line with market trends. This means that bonuses are earned by increasing value added faster than the total company wages and salaries bill. All these points are explained to newcomers to the company, and appropriate explanatory booklets are freely available.

It was essential, if the scheme was to work, for there to be a framework within which value-added results could be discussed and ideas exchanged for improving performance. The forum initially proposed was a single council with members drawn from all sections of the company. However, it was soon realized that because of the detailed nature of many of the topics, this was an inefficient way of working. It was therefore decided to set up six area councils, each one relating to one important part of the company's business. Topics with wider implications were then referred to a single company council. The six area councils set up were:

administration and finance
commercial sales and planning
engineering (research and development)
manufacturing – Beaconsfield
manufacturing – Llantrisant
sales, marketing and service.

Three to six delegates are elected to each of the area councils, each of them representing about twenty employees. They have an independent chairman and include the divisional manager of the area concerned. The company council includes one or two employees from each area council, elected as area representatives by their fellow delegates as well as four managers and representatives of the employee negotiating bodies.

It seems on the face of it to be a formidable bureaucracy, but within the value-added framework, of course, the incentive to co-operate is high. Its justification is in the spectacular results achieved by the value-added scheme. In fact, as well as contributing to the success of the value-added scheme, it probably meets the need for people in any company to get together and talk about the problems and opportunities that face them.

Any action recommended by the Councils is, of course, effected through the normal management channels. If there are any problems, they can be referred by the company council to the managing director. The scheme requires considerable commitment by both management and workforce, but the benefits have been considerable.

Costs have decreased, as a percentage of added value while added value has increased faster than the sales value of output. The workforce now has a major incentive to keep costs under control and they use their best endeavours where they can. The sales value of products has, because of the buoyancy of the market and product innovation, at the very least been kept in line with inflation. The consequence is that added-value bonuses have risen from 3.4 per cent, through 7.1, 8.3, 5.7 and 8.7 per cent to 20.4 per cent in 1984-5. Efficiency has obviously improved, and, by general agreement, so has morale. Inter-union tension has all but disappeared.

There are five important points to be made. The first is that initial commitment in this company came from management. The state of industrial relations had become insupportable and there was an urgent need for improvement. This deterioration provided the stimulus for change. Second, the commitment had to come from the whole of management and not just from the top. There was so much effort required in terms of education and communication that without massive management support it could easily have petered out.

Third, management needed to be exceptionally sensitive to suggestions from employees. A good suggestion scheme feeds on adopted suggestions. As soon as people see that an idea is accepted and put into practice, they will want to come forward with their own ideas. Initially, to create the right sort of climate, it is almost worth accepting ideas that create only marginal improvements.

Fourth, even with a scheme as well-established as the one described, the company found it valuable to introduce briefing groups in 1985.

Once a month, supervisors and managers brief groups of fifteen or so. The previous month's results are discussed, together with other appropriate information. This might be seen as gilding the lily, but it does ensure that managers and staff meet on a regular basis. It provides a forum and ensures that the added-value mechanism does not carry the entire burden of communication. It does not take much time, but it makes sure that company and employees stay in touch.

Finally, the merit of gain-sharing is that it enables employees to receive tangible rewards that are proportional to the gains that have been made by the company through their efforts. It is simple in theory, but requires considerable effort in practice. Over the years, it seemed to bring increasing commitment and reward.

Case 6: Royal Bank of Scotland

At first sight, banks are structured in a way that seems to hinder the creation of commitment. Traditionally, they are bureaucratic institutions, dominated by paperwork and procedure. They are systems-driven and they have to be, so they can handle enormous sums of money; as members of the national money transmission system, there is little scope for individual creativity. Indeed, changes at national transmission level are slow and painstaking, involving not only the member banks, but the Bank of England and the Treasury.

Bank employees, particularly juniors, can be forgiven for thinking that their role is to make the system work and not to ask too many questions. Given the complexity of the banking operation, they may indeed wonder if it is realistic for them to make suggestions that could in any way be relevant to the workings of the bank. Nor can it be easy for many of them to understand the overall purpose and goal of their bank. To them, that is something lost within the arcane mysteries of the international financial markets, beyond normal comprehension.

It is a problem that worries bankers. With the best will in the world, there is little they can do to make the system less bureaucratic. They do not, for example, have the option of developing management autonomy by spinning off a multitude of subsidiaries in which many managers can enjoy the responsibility of being bigger fish in smaller ponds. Even the solutions to the problems of bureaucracy, for example involving staff through the adoption of competent appraisal systems and career-development policies, tend to be bureaucratic. The numbers of staff involved, and the fact that there is a far-flung branch structure, see to that.

Williams and Glyn's, now merged with the Royal Bank of Scotland, has always believed, along with others, that the way forward was through increased staff participation. In fact, their Chairman at the time was a member of the Bullock Committee on industrial democracy, and so it was inevitable that the bank would want to establish some sort of elaborate participation structure. The bank proceeded by setting up a joint working group of members from personnel, senior management and the union (three-quarters of the bank staff were members of the Banking, Insurance and Finance Union). The working group laboured for a year and produced a report that in the best participatory fashion, was circulated amongst all employees for comment. This led eventually to the setting up of what came to be called the Central Consultative Body.

This body had 50/50 membership from the union (or nominated members of the union) and senior management, including directors. It was expanded after six months, with union input being doubled. The union thus had a numerical majority, but in a talking shop that was found not to matter. The bank then tried to set up some sort of involvement mechanism at branch level by asking each manager to hold a quarterly meeting of his unit to discuss matters of significance.

The whole structure had, as far as Mike Mosson, General Manager Personnel, could see, 'absolutely no effect in obtaining commitment to anything'. Despite all the effort and formality, the whole thing was a failure. Clearly something else was required.

The solution, almost accidentally, came through the decision to introduce a code of customer service. Williams and Glyn's had always prided itself on a high standard of service but decided that this should now be formalized through a code. The Marketing Department had discussed with consultants how such a code might be introduced. Initially it had been concluded that an elaborate and comprehensive training programme was required. In the end, however, that path was rejected as being perilously close to the institutionalized bureaucratic approach that had been tried and had so demonstrably failed.

The bank decided instead to introduce the code in its own way. Senior management wanted to develop the code and introduce it to staff in a way which demonstrated management's overall commitment to it. In accordance with the bank's belief in developing commitment through participation, they wished the staff to develop their own local solutions to the problems posed by the code. In making their plans, senior management spoke to a number of organizations, including Marks and Spencer, whose help they gratefully acknowledge. What emerged was an amalgam of briefing groups and quality circles, adapted to the bank's own circumstances.

With one exception, the briefing groups were essentially based on a well-known procedure: each manager briefing his team, and each member of that team briefing his own subordinates and so on down the organization. This system is known colloquially as the grandfather-father-son approach. The 'grandfather' or senior manager briefs his own subordinates or 'fathers', who in their turn brief their own subordinates or 'sons'.

The Bank modified this procedure in that the grandfather briefed the sons *in the presence of the father*. (In the bank's own terms, the managing director briefed the general managers in the presence of their bosses, the executive directors, and so on.) The bank felt that their approach demonstrated without doubt senior management's unequivocal commitment to the code. They rightly felt that it is difficult to ignore something which is said by the 'boss's boss' in your presence. It is an approach ideally suited to the introduction of a major policy change.

The second stage was the introduction of quality circles at unit and branch level. There was some reluctance to use the term 'quality circle', since circles are fashionable and fashions pass. However, it was decided to call a spade a spade, and 'quality circles' was the name used officially. The purpose of the circles was for the staff to consider on a fairly regular basis how standards of customer service in their branch could be improved. It included such topics as how the customers and public could be made to feel more welcome; what obstacles existed to giving a better service and how they might be overcome; what could be learned from local businesses enjoying a good reputation.

There was a very clear brief provided as to the roles of manager and staff. The circles were to 'belong' to the staff, not to the management. There were two major reasons for this. Firstly, there was a significant average age difference between management and staff. The majority of clerks in the branches were in their late teens or early twenties. The managers were anything between 35 and 59 but averaged around 45, so there could be a major generation gap between young employees and their managers. The presence of a manager in a group could therefore be quite inhibiting, and it was felt necessary for somebody else in the branch, not necessarily the next in seniority – or indeed anybody in a position of seniority – to lead the circles.

Second, the bank was organized in such a way that all communication was via the 'manager'. There was no way the staff could communicate with the bank outside the branch except through their manager, and vice versa. Clearly, for the bulk of the business, that state of affairs was going to continue. However, as an act of deliberate policy and as an experiment (and in contrast to what is normally done in quality circles), it was decided to go outside the normal organizational chains of command and to set up circles in which the leader was not necessarily the supervisor or most senior member of staff.

As far as employees were concerned, the brief went on to say that all the staff were to be volunteers, meeting regularly in small groups, and that training would be provided for leaders if they wanted it. Communication from HQ to the circle would be direct to the QC leader. That was a major break with practice for the bank, which actually had to design a new internal procedure to make it possible to communicate with somebody other than the manager!

The role of management was equally clearly defined. Managers were asked to call a special staff meeting to invite, and if necessary to encourage, volunteers to join a quality circle – and to take the first steps by setting a date for the meeting. The manager was to allow the circles the time and facilities required, and he was asked to respond as positively as possible to recommendations; to co-operate and monitor results and to report results up the line and across the organization on a regular basis. Managers were given guidance on such questions as how to respond to proposals from circles involving expenditure for which there was no budget provision.

The managers were also to give a quality circle briefing booklet to a member of the staff so the circle could get started. The brief is fairly basic, describing the aims of the circles and including a suggested agenda.

Inevitably there was considerable variation in the effectiveness of the circles. The best set themselves clear objectives, leading to a systematic examination of the services provided. These included an examination, for example, of how to get the best results from the enquiry desk. Were customers prepared to wait until the right person was available to answer their query, or would they prefer a less authoritative answer from the persons who happened to be manning the desk?

More encouragingly, some of the circles started to look beyond the straight customer-service brief. They examined and reorganized computer work flow and developed better methods of avoiding peaks and troughs. Particular individuals were made responsible for tasks like progressing renewals and applications for cheque and cash cards. Seating arrangements were changed from those that had previously been established by the O & M department, and so on.

All in all, although staff knew they were still working in a necessarily bureaucratic organization, they began to feel that they 'owned' the branch and that there were parts of the organization that they could influence. Although it is difficult always to quantify the benefits, there was agreement on both sides that there had been a step forward in increasing commitment.

Then came the merger with the Royal Bank of Scotland. This was a period of intense and indeed frenetic activity, with staff fully occupied in converting systems to the new order. Attention inevitably shifted, and over a period of two years the circles were put on the back burner. They were relaunched in 1985 under the leadership of a Regional General Manager from the Royal Bank. It is probably too early to give a formal assessment of their overall benefit.

Both constituent banks to the merger had, like many other organizations, wished to introduce employees to the benefits of share ownership. In keeping with these views, and prior to the merger, they had each introduced a profit-sharing scheme which gave employees the option of taking cash or shares. Employee take-up, to the disappointment of both banks, had been on the low side. Within Williams and Glyn, share take-up had reached only about eleven per cent of those eligible in 1984, up from about nine per cent in 1982. In the Royal Bank, share take-up had moved from about thirteen to about eighteen per cent over the same period. Research revealed that, on average in industry and commerce, share take-up was of the order of twenty to twenty-five per cent of eligible employees. The merged Royal Bank decided it should do better.

How it went about it is an object lesson in the benefits to be achieved by effective communication. First of all, the bank had to decide which scheme should be made available. It obviously wanted employees to enjoy the available tax concessions and opted for a conventional SAYE share-option scheme. These schemes are fairly well known: briefly, an employee contracts to save with a building society or the Department of National Savings an amount which is at present between ten and one hundred pounds a month, for five or seven years, after which time a substantial bonus is paid. At the end of the agreed period, he or she can decide whether or not to buy shares in the company at a price fixed when the employee joined the scheme. Savings and bonus can, of course, be withdrawn, instead of used to buy shares.

The scheme does not, of itself, lead to share purchase. What it does is contract employees into a savings scheme whose outcome at the end of five or seven years is share purchase – provided the share price is right. (Given the right price, those in the scheme will benefit from buying. Given a decline in the price, below the level at which the option was granted, there will be no benefit.) Whatever happens, the employees will not lose. If they do not buy shares, they will still have their savings and a handsome bonus. In effect, SAYE schemes take the long view on increasing employee share ownership.

In presenting its proposals, the bank might be thought to have one major advantage: its employees were financially literate and used to reading and understanding complex circulars. That indeed might have explained the low take-up on the established profit-sharing scheme – a view, incidentally, not held by the Bank. But it was clear that the employees had not been particularly motivated by the idea of share purchase. The SAYE scheme provided the opportunity to change that.

The bank decided it would make a positive effort to publicize the benefits of the proposed SAYE scheme. It would take nothing for granted and would give a full and complete explanation. The message would be communicated by line management using the already established briefing channels. The preparation of the scheme, initial briefings of senior management and preparation of briefing material would be undertaken by Cockman, Consultants and Partners, experts in this field.

The approach they recommended was very simple. It was to use prepared flip charts to describe the scheme in outline and to provide notes and recommended answers to the briefing group presenters. The presentation took some twenty minutes, up to an hour with questions and discussion. The average size of each group was about twenty, with most of the presentations taking place in the branches.

The actual presentation was very basic. It started by differentiating between the new and the already established schemes, indicated who was eligible, and then described what was meant by an option. The five-year and seven-year plans were described separately. It gave a simple overview of the four benefits of the scheme, which were: the right to buy in the future at current value; a tax-free bonus in five or seven years; no income tax on increases in share value; and no risk to the saver.

There was then a series of simple illustrations, showing the position in five years' time if the share price improved by, say, five per cent. It described what would happen if the employee left and covered such matters as where to find the current share price (not only in the *Financial Times* and *The Times*) and how to sell shares. The benefits were then reiterated. The programme was a great success. Take-up was fifty-five per cent, compared with the twenty to twenty-five per cent commonly achieved in offers of this kind.

What are the lessons to be drawn? The first is that simple but well-presented explanations are acceptable, even to an audience which is relatively sophisticated. The second is that line managers, properly briefed, are well able to communicate subjects which, though simple in concept, are in fact complex in detail – they were, of course, advised to refer elsewhere for the answer to questions they could not handle.

The most important lesson is that effective communication requires significant management effort. Management needs to think carefully about its message; to take trouble to ensure the message is clear; and then to take time to present it to staff. Managers need to work long and hard if they wish to communicate with their staff. There is no easy option.

6
A sense of excitement in the job: pride

Pride needs to be carefully defined. In the context of commitment, it has no association with inflexibility, nor unwillingness to learn new skills, nor a belief that it is beneath one's dignity to sometimes contribute below one's level of skill. It is certainly not associated with the sort of status-consciousness which hinders effective communication.

It is much more to do with the satisfaction that comes from living up to personal standards, concern for quality, acceptance of personal accountability for results, willingness to be trained in new skills and, on occasion, to keep things going by 'mucking in'. Its overwhelming characteristic is an awareness of the need to contribute to high standards of organizational performance. Pride is often believed to be a characteristic of the professional worker.

The working atmosphere in industry in the late seventies, on the other hand, was generally not conducive to pride. People had not attuned themselves to the more effective methods of working that have characterized the eighties. Industry was significantly over-manned and riddled with demarcation practices.

But if pride has returned today to the best parts of manufacturing industry, it did not come easily. Fear came first — the fear of managements who were fighting for survival and making thousands redundant.

For example, in British Steel, around half the workforce were made redundant. In South Wales alone, in 1980, over ten thousand left the organization. Jaguar took one bite at the cherry and shed forty per cent of their employees at the beginning of the eighties, while Hardy Spicer and Schweppes each shed about the same proportion at various times from 1979 onwards.

The change in the industrial climate was extraordinary. So were the results. There were dramatic falls in overtime and absenteeism. Companies began to report that they were achieving the same levels of output with only half the workforce and that improvements were still being made.

Fear was beginning to be replaced with pride. This did not happen because management was macho. What was happening was more subtle. Because of poor industrial relations and the lack of trust in most organizations, management had no alternative but to act arbitrarily and make severe cutbacks. Once the immediate crisis was over, however, there was a complete change of approach. Management set out to enlist the co-operation and goodwill of the workforce.

They did so for two reasons. Co-operation and goodwill are in principle preferable to confrontation; and both are necessary to achieve continuing effectiveness.

This can be seen clearly in the matter of quality. Traditionally, quality was the responsibility of the quality department. The workers saw their responsibility as output. They adopted an adversarial role in their dealings with the quality inspectors. Quality was not their problem: if they could get away with poor quality, they would. So a vicious circle was established: as quality deteriorated, more quality inspectors were appointed — and so the workers felt even less responsibility.

Jaguar, for example, found that about eleven per cent of their workforce was involved in quality control, and that maintaining standards was very expensive indeed. They certainly wished to maintain and even improve standards, but at less cost. Management felt that quality should be the responsibility of the workers on the line and that such a large inspectorate should not be required. It was therefore sharply cut back and a 'get it right first time' training scheme introduced to move responsibility for quality back to the workforce.

Hardy Spicer reached a similar conclusion. It had one hundred and fifty inspectors to prevent the operatives producing bad work. Workers could therefore always put the blame on the inspectors: 'Why has the inspector let me produce bad work?' The inspectors were replaced with thirty quality engineers. Responsibility for quality was placed on the operative, with the quality engineer there if help was needed.

Both these companies, and other companies who have gone in the same direction, have been able to feed back to the workforce information about the quality achieved. Jaguar, for example, introduced quality tracking, that is, interviewing a hundred or so people who have bought Jaguars and competitors' cars and asking their views about the quality of the product they had bought. Hardy Spicer are given detailed information about warranty claims by the motor manufacturers they supply. Both companies have achieved high quality, and the feedback received by the workforce has enhanced their sense of pride in the product.

TI Raleigh went the same way with their Lightweight bike, an up-market model transferred to Nottingham from the Worksop factory. The bike is produced in a small unit within the main factory, with no inspectors and the workers responsible for quality. Such was the pride developed that each bike now leaves the factory with a photograph attached of the person who made it. The workers clearly feel a direct identification with the product, on whose quality they are staking their personal reputation.

Increased responsibility for quality, erosion of demarcation boundaries and increasing manufacturing sophistication led to another development that increased pride. Industry was having to make a conscious effort to upgrade the skills of its workforce.

There seems to be no shortage of volunteers wanting to be trained. Hardy Spicer wanted to make a major improvement in workforce skills before investing heavily in sophisticated computer-controlled machinery. It had eight hundred volunteers for the initial forty places. Jaguar is constantly working to upgrade employee skills. As part of its programme, it introduced an open learning scheme providing over fifty courses. Twenty-three per cent of employees are now participating. Pilkington wanted to upgrade the skills of existing employees recruited for their new greenfields site; those recruited welcomed the opportunity to learn new skills. British Steel can tell a similar story.

It is almost as though there is a latent urge for self-improvement, which is tapped as companies move forward and increase the demands made on their employees. It makes one wonder how much potential there is untapped in British industry. But there is no doubt that training not only increases competence, it increases pride and enhances commitment.

Companies can improve efficiency by constantly searching around to find best practice and then seeking to match it. In doing so, they develop pride. Schweppes, as it was called before a new company was established following the merger with Coca Cola, was one of the companies that used this approach. Although it operated in a growing market, competitive pressures were intense. Schweppes sought to remain on top by setting out as a matter of policy to match the best.

It had a three-point approach. It tried to identify best practice internally within the company and required other parts of the company to meet the standard set. The policy was backed up by what was called 'resource denial'. Factory cash limits were literally unchanged from 1980 to 1985, though output produced by the factories increased by half.

The approach was supplemented by improvements required from 'fast trackers'. These were factories which should have been able, because of their facilities, to produce at a significantly higher level of efficiency than the others. They had usually not done so because of under-utilization. They were therefore given production from other parts of the organization to achieve one hundred per cent capacity. This led to improvements in efficiency of the order of fifty per cent.

The third focus was external. The company set out to find and match best practice in the world. Finally, close attention was paid to costs achievable on greenfield sites.

A company that sets out to achieve the best and provides the necessary resources and drive evokes a response from the workforce. When Schweppes was awarded the Coca Cola franchise, it could claim its search for excellence had kept it to the fore. Likewise, Burton set out to be the leading fashion retailing experts of the nineteen eighties, and the organization has been visibly successful.

People who work in committed companies are facing the same pressures as the professions: competition is intense; the demand for quality is high; people are expected to maintain and enhance their skills and are held accountable for their work. The same pressures evoke the same response — pride. It is an important facet of commitment.

Case 7: British Steel

'Down but not quite out' – this, not so many years ago, was a fair description of British Steel. 'Lean, aggressive and successful' is the sort of praise it merits today. Over a period of five or six years, BSC has changed beyond recognition. Although it is true that, in a competitive world, it has even further to go, its standing in the international world of steel is high. The transformation is a great story.

Ten years ago, the typical British Steel plant was heavily overmanned. Compared with its Continental competitors, there were at least twice as many employees per ton of steel produced. There were nine or ten unions anxious to defend outmoded demarcation practices. The organization was heavily centralized. Decisions were not made at plant level, they were made in London.

British Steel was a creature of the politicians. It had been nationalized, denationalized and renationalized. The expectations of managers and employees had developed in the post-war era of seemingly unlimited demand for steel, when the future seemed to be bright and governments invested for expansion. There was a preoccupation, in that era of full employment, with satisfying employee demands for better terms and conditions. Making British Steel cost-effective appeared to be low on every list of priorities.

The oil price shock of 1973 provided the first indications that things would have to change. Industry plunged into recession. There was an enormous cost/price squeeze and the corporation started to lose money fast. There was need for an immediate reaction: the old plants had to go, far faster than anybody had ever anticipated, and the modern plants had to quickly achieve manning levels and working practices at least up to Continental standards.

Although management and unions went through the motions, there was no real sense of urgency. Nobody really believed that governments would let things become too traumatic. So the problems were discussed through the National Negotiating Procedures. Head Office senior management met with the national representatives of the trades unions. Both sides agreed National Enabling Agreements whose purpose was to improve productivity. In practice, these led to minimal improvements which were paid for twice – at national enabling level and at local level as well, where further wage concessions were frequently granted. As for plant closures, the government saw them as a political hot potato to be delayed as long as possible.

Unfortunately, while the principal actors in this drama procrastinated, the financial deterioration continued and even accelerated. Every one of the steel-using industries – mechanical engineering, construction, miscellaneous metal goods and motor manufacturing – was in steep decline: the first three, by roughly 20 per cent over a ten-year period and the last, cars, by no less than 40 per cent. British cars, for example, took two-thirds of the UK market in 1970 and had declined to one third by 1985.

The problem, of course, was not only British, it was European and worldwide as well. There was global overcapacity. Price increases were below cost increases, particularly those of raw materials and energy. In the UK, the problem was exacerbated by exchange rate difficulties.

This desperate situation called for desperate remedies. The initial political impetus for change came from the Callaghan government and followed hard on the financial crisis of 1978/79. The new direction was confirmed by the election of Mrs Thatcher.

The Corporation made a number of policy shifts. The first was to push authority back to individual businesses to make them less dependent on the centre and more responsible for their own destiny. Wages would henceforward be substantially determined at local level, though within a national framework. Wage improvements would come through local bonus schemes.

The old plants had to be closed, without union support. Finally, in the words of Stephen Best, Industrial Relations Director, 'There was an absolutely gritty determination that if the Corporation was going to fail, it would be due to economic factors, and failure would not be hastened by problems of overmanning and bad working practices'.

The workforce did not see it that way. In January 1980, it went on strike. On the surface the strike was a classic conflict between a union pay claim, seen as excessive by the management, and a management offer, seen as objectionable in principle by the unions. Under the surface were two perhaps more important issues:

(i)   the determination of the Corporation both to shift the pay bargaining from national to local level and to tie pay to performance and productivity via local lump-sum bonuses.

National trades unions saw this as a threat to their traditionally powerful role in general pay bargaining.

(ii) the determination of the unions to resist the accelerating closure programme. So far only the older plants had been closed. Now, for the first time, new facilities were being threatened. For example, late in 1979, there was a real prospect of either Llanwern or Port Talbot closing.

The strike was, with the exception of the middle managers and managers who were members of the Steel Industry Management Association, all but solid and lasted for three months. During that time, local management started to use its new found relaxation from central control. Its policy was to work out the manning levels and working practices that would be required to run an efficient operation. It decided to look at best practice and to ignore historic demarcation arrangements and outdated agreements. It worked at a very fine level of detail, down to which of their employees could, and would, do what was going to be required of them.

It looked at all departments. It examined the relationship between employee groups: craft, production, ancillary, supervision, technical. It posed questions like 'Now that there are no capital schemes in the pipeline, do we need a drawing office?' If they found they did not, the drawing office was closed. They asked themselves if they could contract out functions like catering and transport. If they could, they did. It was a period for slaughtering sacred cows.

The strike was ended by a Court of Enquiry which recommended that local lump sum bonuses should be introduced as a major part of the pay packet. The settlement was accepted by all parties. The real test was now to come: how would management impose its new vision? More to the point, if it could impose it, how would it gain the commitment of the workforce? Looking back from the vantage point of the late nineteen eighties, it is clear that the Corporation has gained the commitment of the entire workforce. In fact, it has a double achievement to its credit: it gained commitment at a time of terrible crisis – it harnessed the traditional 'Dunkirk' spirit – and, more remarkably, it has managed to maintain it.

How did it do it? It is worth putting that traumatic time for both management and workforce into perspective. For example, the Strip Products Board was responsible for Llanwern, Ravenscraig and

Port Talbot. All three were major steel mills. The Llanwern site is three and a half miles long and one and a quarter miles wide. In 1979 it had a capacity of about three and a half million tonnes and employed some 10,000 people. Port Talbot was also capable of three and a half million tonnes. Ravenscraig had just had a major capital development scheme and could produce two million tonnes; the Corporation wished to use it to the full.

The Strip Products Board was faced with a market that could only take 4.8 million tonnes. Two million were to be provided by Ravenscraig, leaving 2.8 million to be provided by South Wales. The Board was faced with a choice. It could either close Llanwern and maintain Port Talbot; close Port Talbot and maintain Llanwern; or close half of each, making steel in Port Talbot and rolling the finished steel strip in Llanwern.

All three of these options had associated logistical difficulties, and local management developed a fourth option: to run both of the mills at 1.4 million tonnes capacity. This was the 'worst' option in terms of cost reduction but was more capable of being rapidly introduced. It meant reducing employment at the two plants from a total of 21,900 to 10,600 – and doing it fast. This was the option eventually introduced.

The initial cutbacks, at the end of the strike, were accomplished against a background of fear. As one redundant employee explained, 'We knew that things could not go on as they had been. Our wives used to tell us that we never did a full day's work for our money, and they were right. It had to change. People had to go or there would have been nothing left – nothing for anybody. I was sorry to go, but it was the right thing'. Fear was the catalyst. What has grown from that has been pride.

Managers acted with a ruthlessness and determination that perhaps surprised even themselves. They presented their proposals in April, at the end of the strike, and said they had to be accepted by June and implemented by July. The programme was non-negotiable. If it was not accepted, then one of the plants would have to close.

The management approach to redundancy was very tough. Every employee, from senior managers down, was given a choice of two options. They were given their own personal terms to volunteer for redundancy, including ex-gratia payments, pension entitlements and post-redundancy benefits. They were also told, in writing, exactly how their department would operate if they stayed. The statements were unambiguous. There would be flexibility, no demarcation and no obsolete working practices.

Management was not prepared to accept any rote formula for redundancy like 'last in, first out'. That way, there was a danger that good people could be lost. Managers, whilst taking into account those wishing to volunteer for redundancy, insisted that they would make the final choice. People would be selected on the basis of their ability, attitude, and attendance record.

What part did trades unionists play in this process? Did they obstruct or co-operate? Attitudes were inevitably mixed and ranged from realistic and responsible to resistant. Those who resisted went. Those who wanted the organization to succeed, a majority, stayed. It needs to be realized that there were large numbers of people in the plants who resented the inefficiencies and restrictive practices; they wanted the chance to work effectively – and there were many trade unionists amongst them.

The Port Talbot and Llanwern experiences were similar. Success in South Wales, however, put Ravenscraig on the spot. In 1982, after a short stoppage, Ravenscraig underwent the same rapid transformation as the South Wales plants. Teeside, Scunthorpe and Special Steels at Sheffield/Rotherham followed suit.

It was this sort of change which allowed the establishment of a joint multi-union committee in each plant. Within this committee, there was complete integration of the eight trades unions into a single body for consultation and negotiation at each of the works. The localities were achieving what had never been achieved at the centre. All other structures were swept aside. These committees became so integrated that it almost seemed as if there were no advantage in having the unions actually amalgamate.

They became very business-orientated. At Llanwern, for example, the first three items on the agenda are cost, quality and delivery. Managers who participated in the monthly slimline committee meetings came to expect considerable pressure if their departments were the ones failing to meet the current objectives. This system is mirrored at departmental level. There are now far fewer meetings, and the massive consultative structures and facilities for the trades unions have all gone. The slim purposeful meetings that have now replaced them are viewed with favour from top to bottom.

At the three plants, management took three further steps to build commitment. Layers of management were removed. As a matter of policy, management and white-collar staff were cut back as severely as blue-collar. Those managers remaining were given greater scope to make decisions in their own right. Departments such as industrial relations were drastically pruned.

The managers who remained were multidisciplinary: many of their supervisory duties were removed from them and pushed down to the shop-floor, to senior process operators and senior craftsmen. Those they supervised tended to work as teams. They did so to the extent that demarcations had disappeared: not only between crafts; but between craft and ancillary; craft and process; between blue-collar and quality-control and primary recording staff. The amount of training required was enormous. Much of it was done initially by the workforce, on the job. As time went on, training became more sophisticated.

Fewer, more accountable managers meant improved communications. This slimming down of management had one additional benefit. The employees on the shop-floor could see that redundancies affected those higher up the ladder as well. It went some way to sweetening the bitter pill they themselves were having to swallow.

Management's second move was to ensure there was a major increase in the effectiveness of communications between management and employees – both ways. The primary route was the management line. It was a management job to tell employees what was happening. This was a relatively easy task because the level of commitment had started to develop to a very high level. As Stephen Best put it, 'The effectiveness of communication is directly related to the receptiveness of the person being offered the information. If he or she is committed, it is easy, and there are several systems you can employ to get it across, because the employee will seek it out'.

Finally, payment systems. BSC aims to tie pay to locally identified cost reductions and performance improvements. In line with this policy, there were no nationally determined pay increases in 1982, 1983 or 1984. The local bonus schemes were reviewed at local level and led to pay increases that have been at least in line with the Retail Price Index and have generally kept up with earnings in other industries. The bonuses were consolidated where improvements in performance were permanent. The national union leadership has opposed local pay determination, but local union officials have signed agreements even when instructed not to do so.

The local bonuses were paid retrospectively (in the form of a percentage of pay to everybody, from the director downwards) and so related to money actually earned rather than promises given. They were based initially on improved financial performance, though more recently there has been an increased emphasis on profit. No sectional negotiations were allowed.

In 1985, during the miners' strike, the steelworkers (who had all continued to work) were given a 3.25 per cent increase determined nationally and, in 1986, 2.0 per cent, which was to be triggered by agreement on the local lump-sum bonus. Despite this, the bulk of pay increases have been determined locally.

The schemes varied from one site to another, but they all concentrated on the cost reductions and performance improvements required by the particular works. The sort of factors covered are man-hours per tonne; cost of finished products; and delivery of material of the right quality on time. Figures are, of course, updated annually.

The whole approach has been very effective. In 1980/81, 125,000 employees produced just under twelve million tonnes of liquid steel. In 1985/86, almost exactly half that number, just under 63,000, produced fourteen million tonnes.

The dramatic cultural change achieved in those terrible months of 1980 began to secure the future. The combination of sharply focussed management, employee pragmatism and total commitment by all saved British Steel from disaster. The Dunkirk spirit had triumphed once again. The question remained: was it a flash in the pan or could the higher levels of commitment and achievement be maintained? Would everything slip back as the UK moved out of recession and world trading conditions became more comfortable? Would government keep its nerve and maintain the pressure?

The key consideration is the perception of the employees – including management. What do they want out of work and what do they believe is likely to be the future for world steel? Could they realistically anticipate that the 'good old days' of rising demand might return? Could they take the view that demand for steel will stabilize at a level at which modest effort and government support will keep things ticking over? Or would they take the opportunity to work at their present level of effectiveness in return for very high earnings?

The present world situation seems to have limited their choice. The reality they are faced with is frightening. There is a glut of steel in the world. The newly industrialized nations have invested heavily in modern plant and are running at higher and higher levels of efficiency. The United States, taking fright at what it sees, has restricted imports in its markets. Its actions have cost the European steel producers at least two million tonnes in lost exports. Australia, New Zealand and South Africa have restricted imports. The loss of the US market has driven the Third World to compete in Europe, and they are selling very hard in order to obtain hard currency.

The point can be dramatically illustrated by looking at one simple statistic. BSC employment costs as a percentage of turnover are about twenty-one per cent, roughly the same as in Germany. The Japanese employment costs are fifteen per cent of turnover, and the Korean costs are six per cent.

There is overcapacity in Europe, which has led to the need for a quota system which will be maintained until 1988, when free market forces will prevail. This is the point at which it is possible that the European producers will stage a 'raid' on the UK market. The problems seem to be endless, though as the UK becomes a more efficient producer, so are the opportunities.

This is really the key consideration in the maintenance of commitment. The fear that faced all who worked for British Steel in the early eighties has been replaced by pride in its continuing achievements. Where will it take British Steel in the future?

The problem facing both management, unions and workforce in considering and communicating the options is the sheer complexity of it all. And since much of the progress and achievement in British Steel is the responsibility of the workforce, it is important that the situation is one the workforce fully understands.

In fact, although there is a need for an understanding of quotas, capacity considerations, the growth of protectionism, cost/price squeezes and so on, the immediate requirement is to understand the corporation's financial position. For example, a key question is 'Can we reduce our effort now that financial breakeven has been achieved?' Other questions concern viability: 'Does it really depend on increased profitability or will continuing breakeven suffice?'

The message the corporation has to put across is a difficult one. It is that, even at breakeven, there is a requirement for significant cash support to run its business. Minimum financial self-sufficiency requires an annual profit of about £200 million year on year. This is required to meet essential capital developments; to keep abreast of rapidly changing steelmaking technology; and for meeting cost inflation and interest payments. None of this money will be used to increase capacity.

The message, in keeping with established practice, was communicated vigorously by management. The salient facts were established for each division, and slide presentations were made to unions and employees and repeated as required. The message seems to be understood. It needs to be. The facts of international competition mean that the organization is going to require even more flexible, mobile and automated working practices, even higher yields, further savings in maintenance materials and employment costs, and lower energy costs.

Given workforce understanding, management has to provide the tools, both in terms of capital equipment and organizational support. Clearly, all aspects of the business are under scrutiny, and although much has been done, much remains to be achieved. In this context it is interesting to single out training and competence, and pay and employment conditions.

Training is seen as crucial to future performance. BSC has accepted that, despite the spectacular progress that has been made, the quality and flexibility of the labour force generally is at a lower level than that enjoyed by many foreign competitors. As a result, it has undertaken a comparative study of vocational training arrangements in Europe.

One of the findings was that, although overall training expenditure is about the same in Europe and the UK – about 2.5 per cent of employment costs or half a per cent of sales – BSC has to spend half its budget on youth training, while at least one of their main competitors is able to spend almost its total budget on adult training. As a result of the study and of discussions throughout the business it is undertaking a thorough training review. Among other developments, it has set up a small open learning unit and has used techniques such as interactive video which are popular and seem to make a substantial impact on operator performance. Training can be expected to become more intensive, more part of the way of life and more welcome to all concerned.

On pay, the move towards increased decentralization has already been described. There is almost certainly scope for rationalizing the multiplicity of pay rates at local level. This will probably not happen until the Corporation has achieved some financial leeway.

In the longer term, there will probably be a move towards harmonization of conditions of employment. This is probably inevitable, given the increase in workforce skills and responsibilities. As is happening elsewhere, blue-collar/white-collar status-based differences in conditions will become unacceptable to both sides.

The story of British Steel is one of the great industrial stories of the post-war era. It is a saga of tenacity and determination. It shows how the recognition of a common interest between management and workers can transform an industry. British Steel faced up to a mighty challenge, changed its culture and attitudes, and improved its practices and productivity beyond recognition. It deserves to succeed. Unfortunately, such is the state of the world steel market that it cannot rest on its laurels. It needs to do even better. Given its current determination and willingness to change, it has every chance of success.

7
A sense of excitement in the job: trust

Trust is the facet of commitment that comes closest to this book's underlying philosophy of 'faith in people'. There is no better way to build excitement in the job and release latent energies than through trust. If people feel trusted, they will make extraordinary efforts to show the trust to be warranted. Whatever their limitations, they will perform up to them — and beyond — in their efforts to respond.

The 'Pygmalion' effect — the positive influence that expectations can have on performance — is an aspect of excitement-building trust. Most people respond positively to expectations and make every attempt to live up to them. There is no greater satisfaction than achieving something a little bit more difficult than one thought possible — especially when one feels that the effort is appreciated by someone who had faith that you could do it, made their expectations plain and trusted you to succeed.

When people feel trusted, powerful self-discipline mechanisms come into play. That is why their performance is often so much better. Things that are impossible for others to monitor, because no external signs are available as evidence, become subject to far stricter internal controls — known only to the people themselves.

Similarly, peer-group control brings close knowledge of colleagues to bear on collective behaviour. Mutual awareness of operational details is intimate among peers and constant close interaction makes concealment difficult.

Everyone knows what everyone else is doing. Self-monitoring by the group is much more effective than can be achieved by someone checking from the outside, no matter how conscientiously.

When autonomous groups feel trusted, they will exert strong peer discipline on those who are 'letting the side down'. The discipline is often far more severe than any formal 'boss' would care to exert, for fear of provoking an adverse reaction. The group's sense of justice is equally acute.

The group knows each person in detail and the sort of performance he or she produces. Furthermore, they know that they are collectively trusted to produce overall results. They do not wish their performance to be jeopardized by colleagues who are underperforming. Knowing that they have been trusted to make sensible, well-justified decisions strongly reinforces these tendencies.

There are two complementary considerations that have to be kept in mind before faith and trust in people can produce the best results. First, people can be trusted to behave well only if the climate is right. Second, people can be trusted to perform only those tasks for which they have been properly trained.

The abolition of time clocks and/or the introduction of flexitime are examples of trust in the good behaviour of people if the climate is right. We have already pointed out how people respond to fulfill expectations. If it is expected that everyone arrives on time, is there when supposed to be, and then does a good day's work, other things being equal, people will respond. If, on the other hand, there is a climate of confrontation and suspicion, then abuse of the system can be expected.

Trusting people to perform tasks properly or carry out duties conscientiously requires that their ability is correctly judged and/or that they are fully trained to do what is asked. Training is, in fact, one of the major keys to trusting people.

Hardy Spicer realized this when they decided to use their own people to man new equipment that was being introduced. They put a massive effort into training their people on the sophisticated new machines. The basic course lasted six months and was supplemented by trips to visit the European makers of the equipment to see how it should be maintained and operated.

This attention to training resulted in a dedicated group of employees who could be trusted to run the new equipment properly — thus enhancing their commitment and performance.

The more people are trained, the more they can be trusted to do. Pilkingtons, at its new Greengate plant on St Helens, put huge resources (by British standards) — over 2% of payroll — into training its operatives to be multiskilled. They aimed to abolish distinctions between types of technician and have the flexibility of everyone being able to perform all the jobs.

Jaguar puts major resources into its 'open learning' scheme so that people can upgrade their skills. Some twenty to twenty-five per cent of the workforce are following a course in the evenings — on the site and immediately after the shift. This means they are free by seven or eight and still have time for their families. Traditionally, evening courses are later in the evening and involve an extra to-and-fro journey from home to the class, thus blocking more time.

A large part of Jaguar's recovery was built on trusting the work-force to produce high quality. The inspectorate, running at 11% of the payroll, was drastically reduced and responsibility for quality was put on the shop-floor. The 'get it right first time' programme was supported by a massive training and propaganda campaign. Workers are now trusted to be conscious of quality at all times and to be self-policing to ensure that every vehicle is as defect-free as possible.

The beneficial effects of trust and peer-group control are evident in the high performance of autonomous work groups. Shown to be effective many years ago by, for example, work at the Tavistock Institute, their merits are being increasingly recognized. One reason, of course, is the success that the Japanese seem to be having with them, not only in Japan but in other developed countries where they have established new facilities, bought existing ones or formed joint-ventures.

The Swedes, too, make extensive use of autonomous work groups. Pilkington learned a lot from its Swedish subsidiary when deciding on new practices at its Greengate plant. The level of trust they found was extraordinary. Perhaps the best-known example of Swedish autonomous work groups is the Kalmer plant that Volvo built in the early seventies. The car assembly line was abolished and vehicles being built were moved from assembly bay to assembly bay, in each of which a set of operations was carried out by an autonomous work group. After initial teething-troubles, this approach has been found successful — especially in reducing defects and lowering labour turnover and absenteeism.

The Americans, too, as detailed in Chapter 12, are reporting great success with autonomous work groups. Firms such as Proctor and Gamble, General Foods and IBM are reported to be achieving 30-50% increases in productivity by their use. Even the traditionally conservative motor-car industry is moving in that direction: Ford have been delighted with their experiences with group-working on the new Taurus/Sable line of cars.

Rothmans, among our sample companies, is an outstanding example of success with autonomous work groups. Each group's machines are placed around a central area which includes the group leader's office and a tea-bar — comfortable, carpeted and well lit. Each group has twenty to twenty-five members and embraces all the skills required, with the exception of electrical technicians who are supplied centrally.

The formation of groups and their development is supported by an intensive training effort. Group leaders are given, for example, a forty-day modular course, extending over six months, in management skills: leadership, team-building, problem-solving, decision-making, presentation skills, coaching, counselling, planning, budgeting and control.

The groups develop their own internal dynamics. Group leaders, after consultation with members, agree production targets with management. The group is also consulted on crewing, quality standards, materials control and so on. Groups order their own new materials that are held in the factory warehouse on their behalf.

The company is enthusiastic about the results of group working and have spread it throughout their factories. The employees are keen, and every vacancy for group leader has three or four applicants. Results have been impressive. Granted new machinery has been introduced, but 680 people — many of whom a few years ago had never worked in the industry — now produce eleven billion cigarettes a year, compared to six years ago, when 2,200 produced about ten billion a year.

So far we have talked about faith in people, trusting them to perform and so helping to generate a sense of excitement in the job. As we have seen, trust is central to pride and accountability for results — its companion facets in creating a sense of excitement in the job.

A more general use of the word covers the feeling of trust between people within an organization, both horizontally and vertically. This aspect of trust touches the commitment model throughout. Without trust, it is an uphill battle to create a sense of belonging by informing people, involving them and giving them a share of success.

Jaguar would not be able to inform people as thoroughly as it does or disclose such sensitive information to so many people if it could not trust people to respect its confidence. Fears are often expressed about disclosing news that is very good or very bad. On hearing good news, people will start to look for more pay, increased benefits or more leisure. Conversely, bad news will discourage people, blunt their efforts and/or stimulate them to leave. These fears can only be overcome by trusting the good sense of people to take a mature view and put things into a proper context. The chances of this happening increase rapidly the more the company communicates regularly and tries consciously to build up the work-force's knowledge and understanding of the general business environment.

Trust is obviously central to the involvement of people. Without a high degree of mutual trust, TI Raleigh would not have been able to involve the workforce in the way it did when transferring the production of the Lightweight bicycle from Worksop to Nottingham. Management would not have been listening to the workers, and the workers would have been suspicious and reluctant to contribute.

Merely offering involvement and asking for suggestions will not produce a response if trust is absent. Too often in the past, workers have seen their ideas and suggestions brushed aside by a management that pays lip service to participation but behaves as if it had all the answers and the workers had nothing of value to contribute.

Trust is necessary if bonus schemes and productivity gain-sharing are to be fully effective in creating commitment by giving a share in success. Perkin Elmer are aware that the success of their productivity gain-sharing scheme depends on the workforce having full confidence in the financial figures that management present. Furthermore, they have to trust management to judge fairly and quickly implement investment projects that would raise value-added — otherwise the workers will be deprived of potential benefit and trust will decay.

In similar ways, trust plays a central role in creating confidence in management through authority, dedication and competence. Attempts to exert authority will meet resistance in the absence of trust. Every move by management will be seen as an attempt to put something over on the workers. Explanations of competitive circumstances or market pressures will be rejected as deceitful propaganda to serve management's interests.

In the absence of trust, the most dedicated manager will still be on 'the other side'. His efforts will be seen as contributing to his own welfare or that of the company, disregarding the workers' concerns.

The building of trust in an organization is one of the hallmarks of a competent manager. This requires clear goal-setting, sound policies consistently applied and a basic respect for people. A management that is seen as manipulative or careless of employees' interests will not be trusted and cannot be viewed as competent.

Thus we see trust, in a general sense, being central to the model and touching all its facets. In particular, however, trusting people is the vital key to making jobs mean something and, thus, creating a sense of excitement.

Case 8: Pilkington Flat Glass

Pilkington, in 1987, successfully resisted a highly unwelcome take-over bid by the conglomerate BTR. It is believed that the Pilkington defence was enhanced by improvements in performance resulting from changes in its management practice since the 1970s. This study describes the changes and how they were introduced.

Success can, of course, contain the seeds of its own decay. That was the position in which the glass manufacturer Pilkington found itself in the mid nineteen seventies. The company had been operating, since the end of the war, in a world short of glass. It had been able, because of the invention of its revolutionary float process, to exploit that situation to the full. The new process had given Pilkington a significant commercial edge over its competitors, and it had enhanced its income with extensive licensing throughout the world.

As happens so often in these situations, the company had allowed itself to become overmanned. There had been no significant pressure to reduce numbers and this state of affairs had continued over many years . Such halcyon days do not, of course, last for ever. Other major manufacturers began to reach similar levels of technical expertise, using fewer people on more advanced plants, and Pilkington began to become uncompetitive and lost a significant part of its market in the UK.

Pilkington had to change. It was obvious that their older plants could not hope to compete with the modern plants of the competitors. Nor could Pilkington continue with its existing manning levels. The extent of the change required can be shown by the fact that, in 1975, a Pilkington factory was producing 10,000 tons of glass a week with 3,000 people and a Japanese plant was producing 8,000 tons a week with less than 1,000 people. Similar plants existed in the USA and, to a lesser extent, on the Continent, with output in tons per man only slightly less than those being achieved by the Japanese.

There was only one solution: to build a new modern plant to the highest technical specifications on a greenfield site, manned at a markedly lower level. Given the industrial relations history at St Helens, it could be argued that such a site should have been developed elsewhere, where new labour would not be contaminated with old attitudes. However, Pilkington had been long established in St Helens and, it was felt, had a responsibility to the people who lived there. The decision was taken to build a green-field site in St Helens, and to recruit from existing employees in the already established older plants. Lower manning levels and new attitudes would have to be established among people who had become accustomed to old habits.

It was decided to build the plant on land that had been unused for the last thirty years. This area had once housed a coal mine, small chemical processing units and apparently a tea-pot factory! The land was derelict and completely unsuitable for a flat glass plant. It had to be prepared for building by pouring thirty-six thousand tons of concrete into the ground, to fill up the old coal galleries.

The factory planned there was to contain a glass-making plant a third of a mile long. Raw materials would be loaded from a giant conveyor and converted into molten glass by heating at 1,600°C before being floated on molten tin. The continuous strip of glass solidified on the tin before running into a conveyor on which it was cut to size. Any flaws in the glass were detected automatically, and defective glass was returned to the beginning of the plant for repro-cessing. Glass was unloaded by giant fork-lift trucks.

The whole operation was, of course, to be computer-controlled. The operatives were to sit in a large control room watching banks of monitor screens, adjusting conditions in the giant gas-fired plant as required. As is customary in these large-scale modern operations, there would be very few people to be seen.

At the beginning of 1980, half the management team for the new factory had been appointed and given very clear instructions. They were to design procedures and practices that would allow the company to produce flat glass at a lower cost than any of their competitors, and which would carry the company into the 1990s. They were fortunate in that they had as a model a Swedish plant that Pilkington had designed and operated since the mid-seventies.

The major problem that management faced was how to change employee attitudes. The first step was for management to convince themselves that change really was necessary, and to express the way forward in clearly articulated and agreed goals. The second step was to communicate and sell those goals.

The aims for the organization of the factory were established in a series of management meetings. The first of these was that there had to be increased commitment to the job, which would be expressed in lower levels of absence due to sickness and so on. The second was that there had to be increased co-operation between trades unions who had traditionally guarded their own territory and maintained strict job demarcation. The aims were developed in a series of eight points which was called the organization philosophy. Management aimed to have:

1. a single job evaluation system
2. a salaried structure for all employees
3. no indefensible status differences: for example, progression, staff bonus or ability to manipulate pay
4. a level of reward that reflected workforce flexibility
5. no individual bonus schemes
6. responsibility pushed down the hierarchy, making work groups more responsible and accountable
7. a simple/effective/easily understood reward system
8. no payment for overtime.

Management spent two years communicating the message to any-one who would listen. The trades unions believed that manage-ment was trying to move too quickly. In the words of one senior offi-cial, they were trying to 'create an oasis in a desert . Management was convinced that time was not on their side and that change had to be made quickly.

Management really did require an unusually strong sense of mission. It realized that, if it was to introduce new practices, it would not be able to make any progress until it had completely restruc-tured the long-established company/union negotiating arrange-ments, something which the unions were likely to resist strongly.

Under the existing structure, arrangements regarding pay and conditions were decided by a central negotiating group which covered all employees in Pilkingtons, whether they were employed in making flat glass, fibreglass, optical glass or any other activity. Each of the separate union negotiating bodies reached agreement within that central structure without having to consider the conse-quences of the decisions they made on any other negotiating group.

Such an arrangement was not regarded as acceptable for the new factory. Management considered it essential that all the unions should sit down together at the same negotiating table and that all should be a party to any decisions that were made. The that all should be a party to any decisions that were made. The management case was presented to the unions and eventually accepted by them. Their attitude could be summed up in a statement they made: 'We don't like what you are doing, but we understand why you need to do it'.

New negotiating machinery was set up on two levels. First, there was a works' committee to deal with the day-to-day problems consisting of the works manager, six of the site line managers (including the personnel officer and the accountant) and the seven elected representatives of the 400 employees in the factory – three from GMBWU, one from AUEW, one from EEPTU and two from ASTMS. The main negotiations for the site, however, which involved pay and conditions, were to be handled by a joint negotiating committee: the works' committee plus the four full-time officials (one for each of the unions involved) under the chairmanship of the Personnel Director of Pilkington Glass Limited.

The first issue to be tackled was that of working practices. The principle of 'one man, one job' had to be replaced by full flexibility of labour. Traditionally, seven or eight different jobs made up the glass-making department, and each man did only one specific job. In the new factory, management wanted everyone associated with producing glass to be able to undertake any of the jobs involved. Similar arrangements were required for the warehouse, where the glass is cut and despatched to the customer. The most difficult area to tackle was in mechanical engineering, which included fitting, pipe fitting, plumbing, the tinsmith and blacksmith trades, plating, welding, machining and so on, yet the same principle was applied and management wanted every one of these craftsmen to be able to undertake all of these trades.

It was a tall order. The trades unions had jealously guarded each of these as a separate trade and skill over many years. Also, the company had to find men who were willing to undertake such a variety of work. A massive amount of training was needed to ensure they reached the level of ability required.

For example, a typical mechanical craft training programme involved learning new skills such as welding, pipe fitting, hydraulics, use of computers, machining, pneumatics, safety precautions (including use of breathing apparatus) and vehicle maintenance. The formal part of that training took place over seven weeks both on and off-site.

Altogether, the company offered a wide range of engineering

courses. The cost was still, even when most of the training had been completed in 1984/5, running at just under £100,000 a year for four hundred employees. Training was running at a level of just over two per cent of the payroll and is a continuing commitment.

In the event, the people involved welcomed the opportunity to learn and practice new skills, and the new system worked well. The company found that the mechanical craftsmen – as they are called – from every craft acquired sufficient skills to meet all the requirements of the factory. Similarly, the electrical craftsmen's role covered the jobs done by motor fitters, high-voltage electricians, instrument electricians, control technicians and so on.

Thus, by obtaining union agreement to restructuring the nego-tiating structure and by undertaking a major training effort, management achieved its first major goal of job flexibility and inter-union co-operation. Its next task was to create a climate in which commitment could be enhanced and maintained. It established a four-point plan to achieve this.

Firstly, managers arranged to have a regular series of meetings with employees to discuss all aspects of works' activities, perfor-mance and future plans. They decided, as a matter of policy, to be open with all information available to them. This, of course, placed a heavy burden on the foremen and supervisors who had to develop into leaders and teachers – and not all of them were able to adapt.

Secondly, with low manning levels, it was essential, as stated in the organization philosophy, to be able to push responsibility down the line – something which was generally welcomed by the employees.

Thirdly, status differentials that could not be justified were removed. All employees are salaried and paid monthly. There is a common canteen. Holiday entitlement is the same for everyone, and everybody works on average 39 hours per week. Payment was guaranteed and did not depend on overtime or bonuses – though the position on bonuses, as we shall see, was later to change. There was no payment for overtime, but time off in lieu was given instead. The company found that when real emergencies occurred, there was no problem in asking people to come in and work outside their normal shift hours.

An advantage of the no-overtime salary structure was that it became easy to say, for instance, to the six shift mechanical crafts-men that they would be required to provide maintenance cover for the factory 168 hours per week. Provided they worked on average thirty-nine hours per week over the year, they could arrange the shift patterns to suit themselves. They now do so, in fact, without the involvement of the foremen.

The opportunity to create overtime, as existed in the old factories, led to a high level of absenteeism and sickness, running, in fact, at a level of about eight to ten per cent. The abolition of overtime was regarded as a major contributor to the reduction of those levels to two to three per cent. Its abolition also created pressures on management to be more efficient. They were not allowed to compensate for poor planning by using overtime.

Fourthly, there was a reduction in the number of levels of management. For example, Group Accounting had five levels and the older factories had up to seven levels. Management felt that the problem with too many levels was that people could be tempted to do the job just below them – it would, after all, be easier – and there could be significant duplication of effort. The new factory had only three levels of management. Nobody had too little to do and everybody was clear to whom they had to report.

Management made one change, after three years, to the organization philosophy. It agreed to pay a bonus. The matter was considered carefully, because the bonus had to provide an incentive and be simple, easily understood and not open to argument. The last thing wanted was to provide an opportunity for endless negotiation and discussion. Yet there was a strong case for paying a bonus. The plant was designed to produce five thousand tonnes per week and now, when required, produced nearly six thousand tonnes with the same total workforce.

The bonus was therefore introduced in 1984 with the express purpose of allowing the employees at Greengate to share in the success that they were helping to create. It was a site and not an individual bonus and thus contributed to the creation of teamwork. It was based on two simple well-understood measures, the overall yield to despatch and the amount of glass despatched (in square metres) – in a nutshell, manufacturing efficiency and sales.

Bonus is generated if the yield is better than budget, and the demand is greater than design output of the factory in any one week. In practice, the bonus ranged from nothing to £27 per week and was payable twice-yearly. It does not apply to managers. There is one unusual, but not unique, feature: everybody receives the same amount, regardless of their salary – the office girl receives the same as the skilled maintenance engineer. This does not seem to create any problems, and the scheme is regarded as effective and rewarding.

Overall, what was achieved was not easy and there are still some on-going problems. In the words of the Manufacturing Manager, Barry Milnes, 'We anticipated that the problems of introducing such change in a greenfield site would be considerably less severe than trying to make the change in an existing factory or a 'brownfields' site, of which there were five in St Helens. That was the next task'.

In fact, introducing the new practices into brownfields factories was an uphill battle. The company had one advantage. To achieve comparable wages, workers at the older sites had to work about five hours overtime a week. The workers at Greengate clearly had more leisure time. That was an advantage the brownfields workers sought, but they tried to obtain it by 'cherry-picking', that is, picking some of the new practices but not the total package.

The story at every site was different. To take one example: at the Watson Street factory, which produces patterned glass and wired glass, discussions with the unions took place over two years. The company wanted to get all the unions round the table together. It wanted an agreement to which all would subscribe. But it was not going to happen. Whereas the Electrical and Mechanical Craftsmen and ASTMS were eventually prepared to accept the complete package, the members of the General Municipal and Boilermakers' Union, despite the fact that the union was co-operating fully at Greengate, did not want to budge.

The company decided that the way forward was to make an offer to each of the unions separately. The foremen were quick to pick it up, then the tradesmen, then ASTMS. The General and Municipal was isolated. The company cut back on overtime, which it did not, in any case, believe was necessary. So the General and Municipal Union took a vote and by a close margin – 280 to 260 – decided to accept the company's proposals.

So the company embarked on another comprehensive training programme. It expected the task to be difficult. It was always going to be harder to make a change with the same people on an existing site than with new people on a new site, as had been the case at Greengate. The people who had joined Greengate had gone there with their eyes open. Their outlook was more flexible and they had welcomed the different environment. Yet even after nine months, when multiskill standards were not yet as high as at

Greengate, there was a seventy per cent productivity increase at Cowley Hill compared with two years before!

Inevitably there were going to be redundancies, but they were all to be voluntary. Management, however, kept strict control and offered pay-offs only to those it was prepared to see go. There were, in fact, more volunteers than required.

The situation was tougher for the company at the Eccleston Triplex works. In the end, the company gave 90 days' notice of its intention to change working practices. Most of the unions were in the end prepared to negotiate. However, the shop-floor members of the GMBWU were not going to move. At first they would not talk. When they did talk they excluded their own local full-time union officer! Then they went on strike – for eight hours. The saga continued for some time, but the company has now reached formal agreement to introduce the new approach.

The situation at the other plants was similar, though each was in some way different. In the end, all agreed or were expected to agree. What is remarkable about this story is the extent to which even in 1986 there were still shop-floor workers holding out against essential change. It is as though the lessons which had been learned elsewhere in the country had still not been learned in St Helens. Nevertheless, the harsher realities of the mid-eighties were inescapable and management was determined that change would come. When it was imposed, the shop-floor seemed to respond magnificently. Clearly the potential is there. The company's improved performance, highlighted by its successful defence against the BTR takeover bid, suggests management is beginning to unlock it.

Case 9: Rothmans

Some ten years ago, cigarette manufacturers in the UK were challenged to make major improvements in productivity. The timescale they were given was short. The driving force was Britain's entry into the EEC and a resulting change in the way tobacco was taxed. Prior to entry into the Community, it happened that the tax regime masked production inefficiencies. Subsequently it spotlighted them. That tax change, and the changes in the market to which it contributed, has changed the face of the industry.

Rothmans was one of the companies affected. Ten years later, its cigarettes are produced in new ways by a slimmer organization. There have been major changes in working practices, and productivity has been sharply increased. The changes, based on a coherent philosophy of team working, amount to a transformation.

Up to 1978, excise duty, amounting to millions of pounds a day, was paid on raw tobacco before it entered the factory. The labour content of the finished factory product was approximately 4%. Management attention was therefore focused on the material, not the labour. This, together with the pressure for output generated by an increasing sales volume, resulted in a relaxed management attitude to wage demands – for example, a 10% increase in wages represented a 0.4% increase in factory costs.

In 1978, UK tobacco tax was harmonized with that of the EEC. The effect of this was to alter the point at which duty was paid. The factory became a 'bond' – duty was paid at invoice to the customer. Wages now suddenly became 30% of factory costs. People and their problems assumed a new importance.

By the late seventies, Rothmans had two major factories in the UK. The Basildon factory was set up in the late fifties and the Seapark Northern Ireland factory in the mid-sixties. Even in that short period of under twenty years, management's relaxed attitude to labour costs had had the inevitable result. Workforce and unions used demarcation agreements to boost their pay. Overtime was rife and communications fragmented. Tradesmen such as electricians were not supposed to talk directly to process workers — they had to talk through their chargehands. Management did not talk directly to the shop-floor — they spoke through shop stewards.

In many ways what was happening was no worse than in much of Britain's manufacturing industry. At Rothmans, however, the problem was made worse by the continuous increase in output required by an expanding market. This need for ever higher output gave the union stewards a great deal of leverage.

The company's problem was exacerbated by its centralization. This was a direct consequence of the rapid development from one manufacturing facility to two large and one small facility – without a corresponding development of management organization. Anything of importance was decided at headquarters, and managers down the line were starved of initiative. The numbers of layers of management did not help either. The Basildon factory, for example, had nine grades, and many of the managers were, in fact, no more that message carriers. They hindered rather than helped communication.

The change in the tax system coincided with a rising demand for cigarettes, increasing cost pressures and the availability of new cigarette-making technology. The existing set-up simply would not have been able to cope. Costs were far too high and there would have been major problems in introducing new technology and flexible working into existing sites like Basildon. Rothmans' response was to build a greenfield site at Darlington in the North-East of England. Two years later, with demand still rising, they found it necessary to build yet another factory, which was constructed at Spennymoor, a short distance from Darlington.

The layout of machinery at Darlington was different from that at the older factories of Basildon and Seapark. In these older factories, there were long production lines and it was so noisy that it was quite difficult for people to talk. The only real opportunity for conversation occurred at tea breaks or when machines were down for repair. Under the new arrangements, making and packing machines were grouped. Fortunately, the new machines were quieter. Group leaders were appointed, who were given two section leaders and about fifty to sixty staff. There was the beginning of a sense of belonging to a group smaller than the whole factory. What happened at Darlington was a pointer to what was going to happen more positively at Spennymoor.

Rothmans' belief was that the way to get increased productivity and flexibility was to try and utilize the skills they felt were latent but untapped because of demarcation and restrictive practices (and indeed because of the history of centralization). They believed the way forward was to push responsibility and decision-making down the line, and they chose to do this through group working. As Darlington evolved, they worked to establish a systematic approach and decided that the same basic principles should be incorporated into the new factory at Spennymoor. These principles are:

(i)   the basic organizational unit should be the primary work group
(ii)   each group should be led by a designated leader
(iii)   each group should, as far as possible, be responsible through its leader for planning its own work
(iv)   each group should have the opportunity to evaluate the results of its own performance and compare these results against standards
(v)   each group should perform a relatively independent and significant set of activities which cluster together to form a 'whole' task
(vi)   each group should have within it the resources necessary to complete the task.

Spennymoor was the first factory in which the layout was designed to support the group concept: each group's machines were placed around a central area which included the group leader's office, a production programmer's office, a quality-control area and a tea bar for group members. Conditions were good. The tea bars, for example, were carpeted, comfortable and well-lit.

Each group had twenty to twenty-five members, and embraced all the required skills, with the exception of the electrical services for which a group does not have sufficient demand. For an electrician to have belonged to two groups would have breached the principle of group working, so electricians serviced *all* the groups from a central department. Spennymoor had six of these groups in the making and packing area. Other activities from inward stores, leaf, outer casing and outward delivery departments were similarly arranged. As luck would have it, Spennymoor got off to a bad start. There were continuous technical problems with the new packaging machinery. Perhaps, in a way, management's consequent need to address the workforce on the problem helped the groups get established.

At Spennymoor, and elsewhere, both managers and shop stewards had needed to be convinced that group management would work. There had to be a constant effort at team building. It also became clear that the key to a successful group is the group leader. Perhaps that is inevitable: if the company is really going to decentralize, then it needs high-quality first-line management. If these managers are going to be chosen for their 'people' as opposed to their production and technical skills, they must be able to seek advice and utilize the skills in the group.

That is what they are encouraged to do. For example, there was a problem with machine efficiency. Group leaders met with colleagues from the maintenance service group. They had all the facts available, but these were not enough. To get more, they set up an audit operation to get detailed minute-by-minute performance figures for a group of machines. From this they identified the most prevalent causes of stoppages and took appropriate action, repeating the audit as necessary.

So far there is nothing special in all this. What *is* perhaps different is that, as a matter of course, the leaders prepared a descriptive presentation of their aims and procedures before they took any action. This was made to all members of the work group – operators, assistants and general workers. The objective, which was achieved, was to gain the support of them all.

To be effective, this sort of approach requires training. This training will need to recognize that most first-line managers (and indeed many middle and senior managers) do not have basic skills in such matters as group presentation, and usually do not have an understanding of group dynamics. Rothmans set out to remedy these deficiencies by enrolling group leaders on a forty-day modular course which takes place on a part-time basis over about six months. Topics covered include:

principles of group working
team-development activities
presentation/discussion-leading
group discussions
problem-solving/decision-making/coaching/counselling
interview techniques
report writing
planning, budgets, management control systems.

Group managers have total responsibility within the group. Functional specialists are there to support the line role and advise factory and group managers.

The company has adopted an almost messianic approach to group working, and managers regularly attend team-building exercises. The groups are seen to give people a strong sense of belonging and, particularly for group managers, an opportunity to exercise more responsibility at an earlier stage in their career.

The groups develop their own internal dynamics. Group leaders, after consultation with members, agree production targets with management. The group is also consulted on crewing, quality standards, materials control and so on. Groups order their own raw materials, which are held in the factory warehouse on their behalf. Leaders brief their group formally once a month, though, in practice, it was found necessary to lay down times for group meetings in advance – or they might just not happen.

The groups socialize together but do not compete with each other and are not encouraged to do so. Absenteeism through sickness runs at 3.3 per cent, against a local average of 6 per cent. People resist movement from one group to another and there is a great deal of informal control exercised over the few 'oddballs' who do not want to fit in to the group.

The desire to remove barriers between people was emphasized by the introduction of uniforms for all. These are smart and expensive and were only brought in after the employees had been polled. With due allowance being made for the difference between the sexes, the uniforms, as in Japanese companies, are identical for all staff. Managers who wish to exercise their authority are given a real incentive to get themselves known! The uniforms are a rebuff to the idea of management by status.

Group leaders are naturally recruited from within. For every vacancy there has tended to be about three to four applicants. The company wished to extend the internal recruitment pool and offered employees the opportunity of receiving 'pre-management' training. On the first occasion, there were some 120 applicants. All of these received three interviews and were given personality tests (rather than intelligence tests). Of the 120, eight were offered training and, in due course, all were appointed group leaders – including one employee from the accounting department who was appointed head of cleaning!

So successful was the Spennymoor experience, the decision was taken to move to group working at the other factories. But it was not without cost. For example at Seapark, one of the older factories, practically every machine in the factory had to be moved. The new manning levels and operational layout were determined in joint discussions lasting for over a year between management and unions. Out of these discussions came agreement on the need to reduce staffing from 1,500 to 900. This was to be achieved by voluntary redundancies.

This massive change was achieved without a reduction in output or quality. Despite their organizational history, these older factories were able to match the productivity of the greenfield sites. Moreover, within the new organization, the demarcation and differential problems, once a major concern, faded away.

However, since those heady days of expansion, the market has contracted. The decline started in 1985 with the oil price collapse, which sharply reduced Rothmans' prime Middle Eastern market. It has been exacerbated by the growing tendency of countries to demand indigenous production. Some factories had to be closed, and the decision was made, for logistical reasons, to concentrate production in one area, the North-East. The consequence was the closure of Basildon and Seapark. As part of this change, the central organization has slimmed down, and another layer of factory management has been removed.

The period since 1978 has been one of challenge and trauma. The response of the organization has been impressive. Costs per thousand cigarettes have dropped over thirty per cent and are still falling. Six hundred and eighty people – many of whom a few years ago had never worked in the industry – now produce eleven billion cigarettes a year, compared with six years ago when 2,200 produced about ten billion a year.

The production facilities are now in remarkably good shape. There is complete flexibility within a trained workforce, and the company makes a major effort to search out potential managers within the organization. Those who are selected receive planned high-quality training. This investment in people and in training is made with the clear understanding that the next ten years will demand at least as much in productivity improvement as the last. The company is now fully prepared to meet the challenge.

8
A sense of excitement in the job: accountability for results

Throughout our sample of companies, there was a clear tendency to push the responsibility for decision-making down the line and make people accountable for results. This was true for both management and workforce.

A clear management example was at British Steel. Ian MacGregor, on being made chairman, was told that he would probably find it necessary to replace most of the management team. Rather than react hastily, he held his hand until he had time to make a personal assessment. As he subsequently remarked, he found the management to be generally of a high calibre and, in fact, he replaced only one or two senior executives. The problem was that the managers had been bedevilled by constantly changing policies and priorities, never being allowed to exert any local autonomy.

The strike in the steel industry in 1980 provided an opportunity to make a change. The management was told during the strike to use the time to make a back-to-basics review of working practices and manning levels. They were told to produce a plan for a competitively viable steel industry, disregarding so-called political constraints and ingrained restrictive practices. Whatever plan they evolved would be presented to the workforce as a 'non-negotiable' package when the strike was defeated. At the same time, local management would be held accountable for the quality of their plan, its successful implementation and the results it produced.

Giving more local accountability to line management has its price. It means that the centre has to be prepared to grant local management the authority needed to discharge its new responsibilities. It means being prepared to give local management not only freedom to hire or fire, but even freedom to determine the level of reward — or at least exert a significant influence on the level of reward. It also means providing information about performance in comparable organizations, since this supplies a useful yardstick against which management can measure achievements and determine what needs to be done.

Clearly no central management is going to release total control. What it needs to do is to establish requirements in clearly measurable objectives; to delegate financial authority; and to specify those strategic areas where decision-making should be left to the centre. Within the delegated areas, freedom needs to be complete. Local management performance will be inhibited to the extent that the centre insists on detailed intervention.

On the shop-floor, the increasing complexity of technology has encouraged the move to push accountability downwards. People are increasingly doing more than routine repetitive work. Sometimes the work and the equipment are so complex that it is necessary to provide months of training for people to attain the required skills. Such work is frequently too complex to be supervised in close detail. There is then no alternative to making people directly accountable.

In many cases, acceptance of this trend is eased by the fact that technology often provides continuous self-monitoring of its own output. In chemical works it is nowadays possible to measure temperatures and pressures in the remotest and most inaccessible parts of the plant. In engineering works, tolerances can be continuously measured; machines are largely self-correcting and capable of indicating their maintenance requirements. If things start to go wrong, the workers are at least as capable of taking action as their supervisors and probably more capable than their managers.

Even where technology is not so advanced, the increasing need for flexibility and the fact that there are fewer managers around to provide detailed supervision means that people have to be allowed to get on with the job — if not entirely in their own way, at least exercising more discretion than has previously been the case. The only way to operate successfully in such an environment is to have a trained workforce which can get on with the job and to make them accountable for results.

One of the consequences of the move towards increasing accountability down the line is that responsibility for quality is now more firmly a line-management rather than a quality-control function. Since there are now fewer line managers than there used to be, those remaining have pushed responsibility further down. Workers now find themselves with a responsibility for product quality. (If they wanted help, they could call on quality control, but they could not pass the buck to them. The responsibility was their own.)

Giving quality responsibility to the workforce did not mean that management reduced their level of interest and commitment to quality. They could, however, direct their attention to previously neglected areas such as the quality of goods shipped in by suppliers. Jaguar found, for example, that 100% of component supplies in some areas had faults. To correct this, they decided at one stage to allow only one-and-a-half per cent of suppliers' revenue as faults. After that, all faults would have to be paid for. There were initial difficulties, but suppliers' quality soon improved dramatically. Such a decision could, of course, be taken only by management and not by the workforce.

Similarly, Jaguar introduced follow-up customer surveys, and the results were reported to the workforce. In other words, management did not allow workers to operate in a vacuum. They took action to ensure that the workforce had the right materials in the first place and that they were given regular feedback on the quality of their work. Within those parameters, the workforce responsibility was to get quality right.

Another aspect of the trend towards accountability for results, as referred to in Chapter 12 on the US experience, is the installation of stop-buttons on assembly lines. This allows an operative to stop the line, if necessary, to correct a fault rather than allowing it to pass and hoping that inspection will catch it later. Such stop buttons, although used as frequently as is necessary, are not abused. They lead to a marked drop in stress, reduced absenteeism and a dramatic reduction in defects.

Increased care in the gathering and use of suggestions is another aspect of increased accountability. Considerable effort needs to be put into suggestion schemes to overcome the cynicism bred of widespread lipservice to the idea. In fact, formal schemes are not salient in our sample of companies. The important thing is to convince the workforce that its ideas are treated seriously. People need to be presented, in one way or another, with visible evidence that their ideas are welcome and that a significant number are actually put into practice.

Such an atmosphere is also required if quality circles are to flourish. These circles, which have been given an enormous impetus through the work of the Industrial Society, provide workers with the opportunity to discuss ways in which they can improve quality and working methods. They are based on the premise that those who are closest to the day-to-day operations are in the best position to see what improvements can be effected. The circles provide a mechanism for harnessing the creative abilities of the shop-floor.

Williams and Glyn's bank, before it merged with the Royal Bank of Scotland, used quality circles at unit and branch levels. Their purpose was to provide a forum for the staff to consider on a regular basis how standards of customer service in their branches could be improved. All the staff taking part were volunteers, meeting regularly in small groups, with training provided for the group leaders who wanted it. There was inevitably considerable variation in the effectiveness of the circles. The best set themselves clear objectives, leading to a systematic examination of the services provided. Even more encouragingly, some of the circles started to look beyond the straight customer-service brief. Although it was difficult to quantify the benefits, there was agreement on both sides that there had been a step forward in increasing commitment. The circles are being reintroduced in the merged Royal Bank.

Many organizations create commitment in the job by giving challenging assignments that entail accountability for results. Schweppes, through their use of worldwide 'best practice' as a benchmark, were an outstanding example. Organizations of professionals, such as CMG and BDP in our sample, make challenging assignments a way of life. Frequently, the main enthusiasm of their specialists is for their technical field of expertise rather than the particular organization they work for. Challenging assignments are a prime way of maintaining the loyalty and enthusiasm of such technically qualified workers.

Accountability for results is part of the trend towards decentralization and pushing responsibility down the line. It is necessary because knowledge is increasingly located lower in the organization and because there is little alternative as management ranks are slimmed. 'Get it right first time' programmes, quality circles and challenging work assignments interact strongly with pride and trust, the other two facets of commitment in this pillar, to create a sense of excitement in the job.

Case 10: Raleigh Bikes

TI Raleigh, the world-famous bicycle manufacturer, seemed forever to be dogged with bad news. It made serious losses in the late seventies and indeed nearly went under. In the years between 1970 and 1980 it failed to invest heavily enough and, in the apt words of the then Personnel Director, Dick Marshall, 'Large parts of the Raleigh site in Nottingham were reminiscent of the film *Saturday Night and Sunday Morning*'. Management struggled hard to make the company viable and in 1987 it was sold to Derby International, an international consortium formed specifically for the purpose of taking over Raleigh. Raleigh management's achievement, after years of losses, in taking the company to the stage where some-body would want to buy it, was, in the words of the *Financial Times*, 'a feat in itself, especially as potential redundancy costs meant clo-sure was never an option'.

Raleigh's decline started in the late 1970s. The company had been producing around two million bikes a year, but a combina-tion of high interest and exchange rates and problems in the Third World meant that required output dropped to less than one million. The management and workforce seemed to have difficulty in responding effectively to the changed circumstances.

For example, in 1980 most of the direct workers were on an indi-vidual but high incentive-based payment system which had been introduced in 1966. However, three hundred of the workers had resisted the change and were until 1983 paid piecework calculated in farthings! In 1986, this was reformed and the principle of a factory-wide incentive scheme was established, based on 'good bikes out of the door' and costs of production.

There were major redundancies. From 1980 to 1983, the number of employees on the giant 64-acre site had been reduced from 7,500 to 4,000. At the same time there was a major capital-spending programme of some £17 million. A shop-floor computerized material planning and control system had been introduced but had failed to function adequately – instead of help-ing the company's recovery, it had nearly caused its demise.

The background, certainly from the mid-seventies, did not seem propitious to the creation of a committed workforce. There was one part of the operation – Carlton bikes – where circumstances were different and where management and workers together generated an exceptionally high level of commitment. The Carlton racing bike, an up-market machine, had been made in a small manufacturing facility at Worksop, some forty miles away, but production was transferred to the Nottingham site in 1981.

The bike, which was renamed the Raleigh Lightweight around the time of the transfer, is one that will be familiar to semi-serious cyclists, though it is not as prestigious as those which are used in major events like the Tour de France. Nevertheless, it is sufficiently expensive to be hand-made, with a good reputation which was worth maintaining. The volumes produced at that time were relatively low, about 300-400 per week, compared with about 30,000 per week total cycle output in the Nottingham plant.

Maintaining a separate factory at Worksop was expensive. There would be obvious cost savings in moving production to the main Nottingham site. The fear was that making such a move, along with the proposed change of name, would jeopardize quality. The bike would simply be 'lost' in a huge factory whose workers did not have the brazing and hand-spraying skills required. Nevertheless, the move had to be made. The question was how to make the transfer successful.

The approach taken was bold. Management decided to be unashamedly elitist and to select only workers of the highest calibre. It decided that, instead of management making all the decisions, the workforce should be given the fullest possible opportunity to become involved. The workforce were literally shown an empty production area. They were given no promises about wages and conditions of service and, if they pressed the point, were told that management did not yet know the answers. They would have to rely on management good faith. Management helped focus thinking, especially on quality, by inviting top racing cyclists to visit the shop to discuss their needs and requirements.

There was plenty to be done in setting up the new production facility. Machinery had to be brought from Worksop and reassembled, and workers had to learn new skills. Management and workers started to have some interesting discussions, but there was some difficulty in establishing production policy with sixty people involved: after three weeks of general discussion, the workforce formed a small committee which worked with management on the project pretty well full time. The company even flew some of the committee to Holland to visit a factory organized in an approved manner.

One thing was clear to the personnel department – the impetus for full worker participation had to come from line management. Theirs had to be the determination that this new approach would succeed. As Dick Marshall put it, 'There is no way that a staff function, however persuasive, can do the job without that commitment, because somewhere along the line you are going to run into a bleak period when you think you are going to fail. If the person who is managing the department is not as committed as you are, then that is the time when he will pack in'. The lesson for the personnel department is obvious: 'First pick your line manager'.

The line manager chosen, David Bednall, was totally committed to the new approach. He had been in charge of the Worksop operation, and had managed a workforce, many of them South Yorkshire miners, recruited to cope with the rapid expansion of what had then been called the Carlton bike. He had his own views on management, perhaps different from those generally prevailing at that time in Raleigh. He did not think piecework was necessary to good management, nor did he believe that the only way to ensure quality was to maintain a large quality inspectorate.

The issue of quality was of major importance in the transfer, causing considerable concern in the cycling world. The cycling press was unanimous that quality would deteriorate and that the Raleigh Lightweight bike would fail. There was a universal and openly stated view in the marketplace that the transfer to Nottingham marked the end of Raleigh's involvement at the top end of the market. For those involved in the transfer, management and workers alike, it was a harrowing time. The climate of opinion could act to stimulate or to deter. It was by no means clear at the time that the effect would be positive.

The workforce could see the situation and knew that, if the move was to be successful, quality had to be right. They agreed that quality was something for which they had to accept personal responsibility, accepting David Bednall's view that an inspectorate was not required. It is a tribute to Raleigh management that, though such a belief was contrary to the prevailing ethos, they allowed this decision to stand.

The joint committee then had a brainwave which demonstrated its commitment to quality and turned out to be worth its weight in gold. On every bike produced, the workers involved would attach a signed label with their photograph, and a note that the bike was 'handbuilt by craftsmen'. This was a marvellous motivator and the idea formed the basis of a major advertising campaign. There is no better way to create pride than being personally identified with the product one has made.

As a result of generating this personal commitment to quality, there is no inspection in the department at all. The operator is totally responsible. Production levels increased from 400 to around 900 bikes per week, and quality is now regarded by the market as having improved. Product pride is reinforced when people write in and compliment the individual worker whose bike they have bought. When such a letter was received from a Member of Parliament, morale soared. Similar reinforcement occurs from the display of cups and other trophys won by Raleigh Lightweight bikes.

The worker/management committee were heavily involved in deciding on a training scheme. The new job took about six months to learn, but a craftsman's level of pride was required so the company was happy to describe the workers in the department formally as 'craftsmen'. At the end of the training period, new members of the department would be presented with a framed plaque stating that they had completed the training. It was a symbol of pride, again to be used in advertising campaigns, and reinforcing commitment.

The committee's decision on payment systems was interesting. After long discussion it was decided to adopt a fixed-rate measured daywork system – without any piecework incentives. This was unexceptionable in itself, but the committee also opted unexpectedly for much higher differentials than elsewhere in the factory. It consciously rejected the levelling up that had become the norm. Rejection of piecework meant that output standards were required – to be set by the work study department. This was acceptable to the workforce, and work study standards were introduced with considerably less difficulty than under the previous piecework system. Within a few months, the new standards were accepted as providing the required balance between output and quality.

The Lightweight operation rapidly established a momentum of its own, and the outside world accepted that its forecasts about a deterioration in quality had been pessimistic. Morale in the department was sustained at a very high level. Then came a period when morale deteriorated. What had happened was that, as part of reorganization, the Lightweight shop became part of a larger department. The workforce lost its sense of exclusivity and control. Fortunately, quality was maintained, but perhaps it was a close-run thing.

While all these developments were taking place in the Light-weight department, the wider Raleigh operation was facing the problem that the workforce, sharply depleted in numbers to 1,700, was still scattered over the original 64-acre site. To tackle the problems this created, management set up a consultancy task force with members from Raleigh, TI Group and the international management conultancy firm, McKinsey. Following the report, management re-established a sense of strategic purpose and instituted major changes, including the consolidation of production onto one part of the site. They adopted a positive programme to reduce costs to a level which would match the competition and return the company to profitability.

The latest development before the sale to Derby International was that the Lightweight operation was becoming more decoupled from the main Raleigh operation. The reasoning was twofold. First, there are substantial differences in the market for lightweight racing bikes and 'mass-production' bikes. Second, relieving the main operation of responsibility for Lightweight inventory and planning makes sense. In due course, it is intended that Lightweight will produce its own profit and loss account, a move which will strongly reinforce the sense of belonging and pride which is so clearly important to the Lightweight workforce.

Are there any lessons for its 'mass-produced' bikes that Raleigh could have derived earlier from its Lightweight experience? There are, of course, differences in the methods of production. Lightweight operates on a much smaller scale. There are fewer bikes produced, and workers can identify easily with bikes they personally produce. It would simply be impractical, for example, to attach a photograph of a worker to a 'mass-produced' bike – too many workers have been involved.

But some things can be done, and they are happening. For example, the Managing Director and Production Directors personally presented the results of the joint consultancy report to the entire workforce of 1,700 people, speaking to them in groups of forty at a time. Giving the same presentation some forty times is surely a tour de force and clearly demonstrates management's commitment to communication. Similarly, a real attempt is being made to decentralize the main factory operation so that people will belong to units that are more self-sufficient.

A previous managing director had used videos to communicate with employees, and his presentation had been topped-and-tailed by the local manager or supervisor. However, when this managing director left, the meetings had been discontinued. Uncertainty about the company's future was one of the reasons but, nevertheless, this led to some scepticism about management's commitment to communication. Briefing the workforce in such circumstances is extremely difficult. Now briefing groups on a six-weekly basis have been introduced for all employees.

It seems to us as well that the TI Group had acted as a 'benevolent banker' to Raleigh, and that financial support from the Group had reduced the company's understanding of the real need to change. Old habits had perhaps lingered on longer than they should have done. The present purposeful climate in the company suggests to us that this is no longer the case. If not, the company is well poised to recreate the commitment which is so evident in Lightweight.

There is, however, one useful lesson for personnel managers that arises from the Raleigh experience. From time to time, marketing would arrange a large conference at which dealers from around the world would be wined and dined and shown a superb piece of promotional theatre with an exhibition and tours around the factory. In addition, Raleigh would arrange for dealers attending the conference to receive discounts from all the local shops.

Since such events took place in the new era of emphasis on commitment, the company ensured that all employees were included: they saw the same promotional theatre, visited the exhibition and toured the factory. The company also arranged for employees to enjoy, for the duration of the conference, the same discounts as were available to the delegates. Such an arrangement led to a noticeable improvement in morale and goodwill.

The message is that training and marketing together can do much to meet management objectives in terms of building employee commitment. Training departments all too often, when compared to marketing and sales, are relatively impoverished. In Raleigh, for example, marketing could easily and happily justify expenditure of half a million pounds or so on a dealer conference. The marketing budget, at little or no extra cost to the company, can be harnessed to the twin objectives of creating business and creating commitment.

This, together with a policy of trusting employees, giving them the opportunity to contribute to the management of their workplace and making them responsible for the quality and standards of the work, can do much to help a company, if not prosper, at least survive in a world in which volatile markets and heavy competition make the going difficult.

There appears to be no doubt about the success of the Lightweight operation. The bike is doing well, and its future seems to be assured. The new consortium has been given a firm foundation on which to build, and the future looks bright.

9
Confidence in management: authority

Since the end of the seventies, managers in industry have rediscovered their authority. Before that, it seemed as if a large part of management authority had been surrendered to the militants and the unions. In extreme instances, managers could not even go on to the shop-floor without the permission of the shop stewards. Certainly managers could not speak to their workforces about policy matters — they had to speak to the unions, who passed on management's message. Sometimes, as in the newspaper industry, management could not even recruit its own workforce.

That sort of general loss of authority is still evident in parts of the public sector and in those parts of the private sector not yet exposed to the full force of competition. It is still possible, even today, to sit in the office of a general manager, as we have done, while he waits anxiously to speak to the union convenor before making a minor decision. It is still possible to have discussions with some public sector managers as to whether or not they would be wise to bypass the unions and talk directly to the shop-floor.

By and large, however, managers in industry today have recovered their authority. They seized it back when it appeared that, if they did not take the initiative, their organizations would face loss of markets, continuous decline and eventual bankruptcy. British Steel, Hardy Spicer, Pilkington and Rothmans are such cases, covered in this book. In those companies, managers ceased to be the prisoners of prevailing circumstances and took control. All of them have sharply improved their financial position and are now clear about their future direction.

The reassertion of management authority was, in some cases, accomplished rather abruptly. At British Steel, for example, the climate of fear after the collapse of the strike in 1980 provided an opportunity for reform in a 'non-negotiable' package. Optimum manning levels were specified, and a union co-ordinating committee imposed to settle any demarcation problems that these might cause. Redundancies would not be on the traditional basis of 'last in, first out', but decided on the basis of the individual's record for ability, time-keeping and absenteeism.

It is a paradox of participation that a change to a new way of behaving often has to be accomplished in an authoritarian way. Doing this does not necessarily mean that management is fundamentally authoritarian. Nor does the use of a crisis to initiate change mean that management is wedded to the use of fear as a regular control mechanism. In our view, as explained in the last chapter, it is more likely to be the only way out available to a management that has rendered itself helpless by progressive abdication of authority and other poor management practices.

Similarly, the reassertion of management authority does not mean that management seeks to impose an excessively authoritarian strait-jacket. Although there undoubtedly are managers in Britain who believe in the 'macho' approach, they were not in evidence in our sample.

Once it has regained its authority, management can devote itself to its vital functions of overall direction-setting and decision-making, while allowing the maximum possible participation and integration of the workforce.

Management is insisting on speaking directly to its workforce, as explained in Chapter 3. This opening of communication channels is not designed to destroy the shop-stewards but merely to ensure that they are not allowed to stand as a barrier between manager and subordinate.

Reassertion of management authority does not mean that the wishes or ideas of the workforce will be ignored. On the contrary, the greatest possible involvement of the workers will be encouraged, as we saw in Chapter 4. Their opinions and advice will be sought and frequently acted upon. Where, however, there is a difference of view, management will not feel inhibited from making a decision, based on its broader perspective and overall responsibility to all stakeholders.

This clear concept of management's ultimate responsibility and its protection of the authority to act is important to successful participation. Too often, the impression is allowed to spread that all management decisions are subject to worker approval and that nothing, from the most trivial to the most far-ranging, can be done without full consultation, participation and the right of veto. This raises false expectations and, almost always, leads to a sense of disillusionment. People resent being given the impression that they are consulted if it is quite obvious that management is going to make its own decision regardless.

Thus, the approach being taken by the companies in our sample is to insist on authority in the things that must remain under their control but to otherwise allow as much involvement and participation as possible. This is similar to the eighth, or 'loose-tight', principle of excellence in Peters and Waterman's book. Management decentralizes as much as possible, allowing maximum local autonomy and participation, but keeps tight control of a few critical variables.

It must be recognized that, in many organizations, management was pushing against an open door when it sought to regain authority. Workforces throughout industry had seen for themselves that the old ways did not work and had no future. They knew that if they were not prepared to remove demarcations and restrictive practices and raise productivity, they would be overwhelmed by competitors from around the world.

Trends in the overall industrial relations scene in the UK have reinforced this move towards realism. The oil-price shock in the early seventies, run-away inflation, the three-day week and the winter of discontent showed how bad things could get. The collapse of the steel strike in 1980, the restoration of discipline at British Leyland and the defeat of the miners in 1985 showed that decline was not inevitable and that apparently hopeless causes could be won.

Authority that is acceptable to the workforce can more easily be exercised in a non-directive manner: management concentrate on the wider issues and leave much of the detail to the workforce. In Pilkington's Greengate works, the mechanical craftsmen are only required to give the necessary cover and can arrange their shift rotas to suit themselves. In Rothmans, the group leaders negotiate their production workload with top management and then decide with their teams how the output will be achieved.

In practice, the only way to exercise authority today is through a well-thought-out policy of participation, not only because so many people are better educated and informed and *do* have something to contribute, but because even those people who are not better educated and informed *feel* so, and feel they have something to contribute. The social and political climate is such that people feel they have a right to be consulted. Managers ignore this at their peril.

As authority is re-established and responsibility for more routine matters is passed downwards, management has more time to manage. Less effort is needlessly dissipated in the pointless tasks that lack of authority has allowed to multiply.

There is no need to spend time and energy organizing six people to do a job that in reality requires only one; there is no need to spend time haggling about piecework rates; there is no need to spend energy trying to respond to fast-moving markets with a doggedly inflexible workforce. It is possible now for managers to think instead of the real requirements of the job. The much improved fortunes of the companies in our sample show the benefits of this redirection of management energies.

In such a climate, far from tolerating the mediocre, management has been able to introduce best-practice policies. Schweppes, as it was called before the merger with Coca-Cola, is one example of such an organization. Management set out systematically to identify best manufacturing practice throughout the world, both within Schweppes and within the industry. The comparative studies focused on comparable elements of production, thus ensuring there was no scope for explaining away any differences that were found. The results of this comparative work were, where relevant, built into budget assumptions. Managers and departments were encouraged to produce plans showing how best-practice targets were to be achieved for their particular part of the operation. Such an approach is a far cry from the days of demarcation and restrictive practices.

Given the improvement in relations between management and managed, brought about by a proper approach to authority, change becomes easier. Instead of no change until it is almost too late, and then massive and painful upheaval — characteristic of the seventies — incremental change becomes an option. It becomes possible, as at CMG, for example, for management to float the need for organizational change without knowing the details. The expressed concerns of the workforce are then taken into account, and the details of the plan are formulated. This is a stressful procedure but results in a better plan; there is a high degree of commitment since a feeling of 'ownership' is strong.

In summary, management has reasserted its authority and established a new climate in industry. Although this was frequently done abruptly, it was not in a spirit of 'macho' repression. The reassertion of authority in crucial areas has allowed management the time to focus on critical questions and has provided a sound base for widespread involvement and participation.

Case 11: Schweppes

Schweppes and Coca Cola launched a joint venture company at the beginning of 1987. This case study describes Schweppes strategy from the end of the seventies to the time of the merger.

Schweppes operated in a growth market. The demand for soft drinks was (and still is) on the up and up. But competition was (and is) ferocious. The pace of change was every bit as fast as in the world of high technology, with constant innovation and changes in practice needed to accommodate increased competition and downward pressures on costs. Soft drinks, like many high-volume/low-margin industries, is one in which it is all too easy to slip behind. A bit of the market is lost here, a bit there, results deteriorate and the cost of recovering profit and market share turns out to be very expensive.

The pressures became overwhelming in the late seventies. Schweppes rose to all the challenges, and in 1986 had so improved its situation that it entered into a joint venture company in the UK with Coca Cola. The new company was born in January 1987. It is now busy meeting the challenges of the late eighties, using basically the approach that served it so well in the seventies.

What was the Schweppes approach? How far was it similar to that of the other companies and how far different? How did it gain workforce and management commitment? The approach started with the assumptions that management made about the future facing the company.

These were that:

there would be no recession in market growth
there would be continuous pressure on prices and performance
competition would continue to grow
the trend to high volume, low margin would continue
the pace of innovation in the market would continue.

Schweppes faced the challenge by first of all redefining its strategic mission. Management looked at where the company was now and where it needed to be. In 1979, Schweppes was predominant in mixers (e.g. tonic). In fact the company was perceived as a mixer business. It was number two in Cola and was simply not poised to participate in the coming packaging revolution. It was cost-heavy and starting to become uncompetitive in price. The business was

not really facing up to a radically changing market. If things continued unchanged, the company could well go into a gentle decline.
The new strategic mission stated that Schweppes would aim to:

> move from being a predominantly mixer-based company to
> become a total soft drinks company
> become the lowest cost supplier of branded soft drinks in the UK
> become and be seen as the leading UK soft drinks company.

What followed was the familiar story of the late seventies – i.e. site
closures, redundancies, increased mechanization, greater utilization
of assets and a push for volume growth. The number of factories
went down from ten in 1980 to seven in 1985, the number of depots
from forty-five to twenty-seven. The workforce decreased from 5,300
to about 3,300. Three more depots were closed in 1986 and one
more of the factories.

In line with best company practice, Schweppes worked very hard
to lessen the impact of redundancy on its employees. There were,
for those employees both willing and able to move, generous sever-
ance payments, and the company facilitated transfer opportunities
by paying all relocation costs.

The rationalization programme was based on principles similar to
those used by scores of companies in those difficult times – to
achieve a reduction in fixed costs, particularly in manufacturing; a
sales volume increase; and an improvement in operating efficiencies. What was in fact achieved over a period of four years to 1984
was an increase in investment of 34 per cent, and a reduction in
manufacturing and distribution costs of six percentage points. The
costs of running the factories' administration and overheads went
down by three and a half points while production, in litres, also
increased by 40 per cent. Trading profit per employee increased
from £2,000 in 1980 to nearly £5,000 in 1985. The market grew by 17
per cent in volume and Schweppes by 40 per cent.

A feature of this approach, particularly in manufacturing, was the
definition, wherever possible, of budget objectives in terms of what
the management called 'best practice'. Management searched
out opportunities for performance improvements by identifying best
practice in plants within Schweppes; by comparing Schweppes performance with that of other companies within the industry; and by
some computer modelling.

The first way, internal comparison, is subdivided into best practice
and 'fast tracker' objectives. Managers identified best practice

within Schweppes and made that the target for budgeting. Thus, for example, if the search showed that one factory was producing 12 oz cans at a lower cost than others, that information was made generally available and became a target. Plants not performing at that level were able to produce plans showing if and how the target could be achieved. They were encouraged to do so by the facts that best practice was built into budget assumptions, and that cash limits were set. These cash limits were so successful that, in the five years to 1985, the overall manufacturing budget was not increased, although production in litres increased by about half.

This approach was supplemented by improvements required from the fast trackers. These were factories which, because of their facilities, were capable of producing at significantly higher efficiency than others. Their frequent complaint was that they were held back because their utilization was too low to achieve maximum efficiency. To test this, they were offered production from other parts of the organization, so that they were able to achieve closer to 100 per cent utilization. This often resulted in major – 50 per cent or more – decreases in unit costs, proving their point and establishing a new benchmark of best practice.

Each increase in efficiency was at the expense of other lines and led to more site closures. On balance, the total operation benefited, and the message about the importance of best practice was showing through.

The second focus of attention was on external comparisons. The company sent teams of managers to search out best practices in other factories in the UK and abroad. They looked for 'elements' of best practice rather than for information about overall performance. In that way they were able to produce specific examples of best practice which could not be explained away on the grounds that like was not being compared with like. The results of this comparative work were also built into budget assumptions and became part of best practice requirements.

Lastly, there was some greenfield analysis. The assumption was that, because the market was growing, it would be attractive to new entrants. The questions asked were: What factories would these new entrants build? What equipment would they use? How would they go about distributing their product? What would be their manning level? The answers to these questions indicated the levels of efficiency likely to be achieved by new entrants. These would inevitably become tomorrow's 'best practice' targets. Thinking about them ahead of time, instead of waiting for them to start hurting, is the beginning of a proactive strategy which is far more effective than continuous reactive defence.

The pressures on management to raise efficiency so dramatically were, of course, considerable. They were helped, however, by the obvious commitment of the company to raising its level of performance. Thus, although targets were very demanding and might have been thought of as impossible a few years ago, managers did know that investment would be made available as required.

Derek Williams, Managing Director of Schweppes and now of the new joint venture company, describes the old reactive approach: 'There were times when we used to pull a washer out of this factory, and a labeller from another, assemble them in the corner of another factory and put on a night shift and so on. These things were done under the heading of "scratch lines". They are now dead. Half measures are usually hopeless. We would be far better off to go and buy from the contract packers'. He neatly summed up the new viewpoint in the catchphrase: 'Scratch philosophies are for fleas'.

Of course, the company's forceful approach could have created morale problems for those working in the less-favoured factories, or in those parts of the organization which were low on the investment priority list. In recognition of this, all were encouraged to find best practice in their part of the company. The results of their efforts were then made available throughout manufacturing and again became best practice.

In 1987, Schweppes and Coca Cola launched their joint venture company in the UK, giving it the opportunity to put together their combined assets and the best brands, together with greater resources and marketing funds. They aim to make both the company and the soft drinks market grow. The goals the new company set itself ensure that the opportunities for best practice are limitless.

Case 12: Burton Group

The Burton Group of fashion retailers is another example of a company in deep distress which was turned round by management to become a leader in its field. Its problem in the mid-seventies was that it had lost its way. It had moved from a profit of about £10m in 1973 to a loss of about £5m in 1977. Following its turnaround in 1978, its profits rose steadily until they reached £82m in 1985. In 1985 it took over the Debenhams Group of department stores.

What was the problem? The company effort was straddled across a wide range of markets. It was not only in clothing, both as manufacturer and retailer, but in camera and hi-fi retailing, in stationery through Rymans, in department stores via Browns of Chester, in mail order and in all sorts of other peripheral businesses. None of these businesses was being run properly.

But even in its own core clothing market it was in trouble. It had failed to recognize that made-to-measure suits, a product on which the group was founded, had been hit by customers wanting more relaxed casual clothes and ready-made suits. The group appealed mainly to older men who were in a minority of spenders and who regarded made-to-measure suits with less and less favour. In addition, other chain stores had moved into menswear, and their economies of scale helped them establish a competing market share. There was only one success story: the womenswear retailing chain, Top Shop, run by Ralph Halpern.

In 1977, in response to the appalling results and to criticism from shareholders, staff and customers, the Burton management invited Halpern to head up the group and put the business right.

His first action was to analyse its strengths and weaknesses. Its strengths were clear enough. Burton was a very well known name. The group owned most of its 600 high-street properties and it was in a clearly defined and profitable market. True, its market share of 4 per cent was low, but that gave it a big opportunity. It had a further strength in that it had loyal and experienced staff. They could help pinpoint the weaknesses. Halpern and his team decided to enlist their support.

He and his team spent a large part of the first two months going around the country holding regional meetings with each of the Burton branch managers. They asked the managers to describe what they felt was wrong and what needed to be done.

In Halpern's words, 'It was a sad, painful and very tedious experience. They poured out years of frustration. Nobody had ever asked their opinions before and if they had, nobody had ever effectively acted upon them'.

The overall picture was depressing. There was low staff morale; time-consuming administrative systems; out-of-date shops and a stock and sales information system that did not work. Bespoke was declining fast, with no successful alternative available. They had no clear idea who the customers were.

The board reported back fully to a management conference some six months later. They gave the managers their findings, exactly as they had been reported to them, and their plans for the future. However, before they did so, there were some important explanations to be given about branch closures.

In July and August of 1977, before Halpern's takeover, fifty-seven small, unprofitable branches had been closed. However, that had not stopped the terrible financial losses. The new board was therefore obliged to announce further closures. How was it possible to talk of a bright future with redundancy in the air? Halpern gave a full explanation, assuring the managers that the closures announced affected only those shops which, no matter how well developed or modernized, could not possibly provide an adequate return under current trading conditions.

He added that such closures were a last resort, and were used when no other alternative existed. He assured managers that, if they were prepared to play their part in the successful implementation of plans agreed with them for their branch, they could look forward to a developing business and a good future.

He said that much of the managers' advice had been built into the group's strategy. He asked them to continue to give advice: 'Only by listening to each other's opinions will we be able to agree on the right way to make Burton successful. So if you have a problem getting things done that you think need to be done, take it up straight away with your Area Manager . . . If for any reason that problem becomes serious because you have not been able to resolve it with your Area Manager, or he has not been able to resolve it – do this: ring me and tell me directly what is going on. If you are wasting my time, I will tell you straight. But if you are right, I will act immediately. In either case, I will listen'.

He then set out the board's view of the company's mission. He said the board had decided that Burton should aim to be the retailing fashion expert of the 1980s. They saw there the opportunity to take on the chain stores and the multiples, and to develop into other segments of clothing for which the group was not at present catering. The implication was that the non-fashion parts of the business would have to go, and in due course all of them were sold off.

Their second task was to define clearly what the group's position should be within the chosen market. In which area of the market should it specialize? The group was mainly in menswear, but women spend twice as much as men on clothes, so clearly there should be a move into that part of the market. What kind of women, though, and what kind of men?

It had to be accepted that the Burton shops, ranging from 1,000 to 3,000 square feet at the time, were not as big as Marks and Spencer, who were able to offer a wide range to everybody. They had to have a narrow focus rather than a broad one. For example, in menswear, they could not retail young and mature clothing in the same store because there was not the space.

There was a clear gap in the market for young menswear, then worth about £800m a year, and Burtons were not taking any of it. So they created, quite separately, Top Man, which caters for men between 15 and 24 and is today the market leader. That left Burton's Menswear free to concentrate on the over 25s. This careful positioning was to be an important factor in the development of the group, and was repeated with a chain for women over 30, called 'Principles', and so on.

Halpern's next move was to set up small specialized management teams. The aim was to ensure that each executive concentrated his attention upon single and simple objectives. This is similar to what happens in other major retailers, but it meant, for example, that in the purchasing department there were buyers concentrating on single products like sunglasses. More important, there would be divisions of only five shops, say, with a finance director, who would be left free to concentrate his efforts on ensuring that the chain increased from five shops to two hundred.

Such singleness of purpose, of course, creates its own problems. How would the left hand know what the right was doing? How would all these finely focused minds be co-ordinated? Halpern set out to solve the problem and to kill two birds with the one stone. His basic approach, to set targets, was not exceptional. He then tied the targets to bonuses; what was novel was that no bonus was earned unless the division exceeded its challenging profit target. This, of course, encouraged the teamwork so essential to the success of the business.

In his view, such targets had to be realistic, rewarding, challenging and self-financing. They had to be so designed that people could not earn large bonuses simply by setting themselves targets which were easy to achieve. If they were to be individually based, they had to ensure that they did not create divisional disharmony, with each employee fighting his own corner in disregard of the overall interests of the business unit.

In addition, if plans were to play such an important part in the development of the business and in the rewarding of employees, they must be more than extrapolations of last year's figures. In fact, the planning process is taken very seriously. The annual plans take each division at least two months to draw up and are based, as in any good company, on extensive information about market trends, competitors' activities and so on. Again, as in all good companies, managers at all levels are involved in building the plan, setting targets and so on.

What was different was that Halpern decided formally to operate two plans simultaneously for each business: *a fail-safe profit plan* with levels of sales and costs to match what management believed could reasonably be achieved; and *a target plan* that was really challenging, with out-of-the-ordinary individual rewards for its achievement. Both plans were formalized and are now part and parcel of every division's everyday strategy: targets at every level down to the shop-floor are linked to the target profit plan.

Bonus is only paid if the division's challenging profit target is exceeded; it is financed by the gap between the fail-safe profit and the target profit – that is, the bonus is self-financing. The bonus available for achievement is extraordinary and can amount to 100 per cent of a salary which is already, in industry terms, highly competitive. However, if the division fails to meet its profit target, no bonus at all is paid – described as 'sudden death'.

Halpern is a great believer in giving high rewards to staff who have achieved targets for which they are clearly accountable. In his view, there has been a cultural change which makes such high rewards acceptable. In other words, high rewards now motivate more people than they would have done fifteen or twenty years ago. He believes that the various share participation and option schemes available are in themselves great motivators, and the company has introduced such schemes at all levels. Allowing people to share in success, for Halpern, is a great motivator.

The question which then arises is: how can a company like Burton institutionalize change? How can it avoid drifting along until it faces some great crisis and then finds itself having to make traumatic efforts to survive? The answer can never be completely known. A company may think it is changing but then find itself overtaken by events. What it can do is set up a process to institutionalize change, and hope that it heeds the warning signals. Burton use both internal and external resources to focus attention on the ever-increasingly rapid changes that are happening in the UK. Market research and market intelligence about competitors are part of this regular feed-back of information.

The management philosophy is that people are trained and motivated to plan for change. Every senior job has change built into its accountabilities and targets. Change is always on the agenda of every divisional board meeting, and the senior management responsibilities for change are formally reviewed in each and every month.

It was out of such a review that the plan to take over the Debenhams Group was conceived. Burton was already showing itself capable, in London, Liverpool and Edinburgh, of managing larger stores. In the directors' view, the Debenhams chain of sixty-seven stores could be made to perform at a higher level. It would enhance Burton's core business and add related businesses like home fashion, which the board felt confident of developing. There was, as well, a successful credit-card operation that would complement their own credit-card business. The 'mission' of the chain would be to provide fashion for the person and for the home.

The acquisition of Debenhams was seen by Burton as an important business opportunity. The takeover was not, however, uncontested. It received considerable media attention and was fought out in full view of the public gaze. The Debenhams board struggled for three months to maintain its independence, but it conceded defeat in August 1985. For the Debenhams staff it was a difficult time. Who knew what the future would hold? Would there be job losses?

But there was a challenge for Burton too. It had to build a new business and had to take the Debenhams staff with it. The problem was that, as well as reassuring staff, there was an immediate need to increase Debenhams short-term profit. The sheer pressure of events made it difficult, at that early stage, to engage in a hearts and minds campaign.

Burton took the obvious immediate steps. There was a full statement by Ralph Halpern in *Debenhams News*. He said that Debenhams stores were set to become the best in Europe. There would be exciting jobs and successful careers, higher salaries and more valuable bonuses. People should forget insecurity. Their future was in their own hands.

But the immediate pressure, as seen by Burton, was to assure profitability by installing Burton concessions in Debenhams stores. This they did – and so helped achieve the £60 million profit to which the Group had become committed.

Despite the frenetic activity, Burton organized three regionally based briefing sessions in November, with one-third of Debenhams management being invited to each. At about the same time, there was extra encouragement for Debenhams staff. Two out of the three new merchandising managing directors were appointed from amongst Debenhams management as was the assistant managing director, stores operations, while the Debenhams Financial Controller remained in his post.

Then there was the decision to undertake a major refurbishment of the Oxford Street store. This continued trading while builders worked twenty-four hours a day to ensure it was ready by the end of 1986. The pace was fast. According to Bob Falconer, retail operations director, Burton was trying to accomplish in that store in five months what would normally take eighteen months.

In February, there were about a thousand job cuts, necessary because of the pressure to contain costs. Sad though these were, they were at least taking place against a climate of expansion. Things were looking set to get better rather than worse.

In May of 1986, over a period of some weeks, Ralph Halpern spoke to every manager, going further into the group mission statement and into what was called the enlivenment programme, which aimed to highlight features of stores. There were many questions, and Halpern answered them all. The mission statement, as always with Burton, was the key which would guide the group's future, and which would provide the foundation for decision-making. An immense amount of board time and effort went into the finalization of the statement. Even against a background of time pressure, there was input from senior management and staff councils.

The mission statement consisted of some nine short statements. Short they may have been, but they spawned twelve task forces. Each of these was devoted to examining the implications for the group of each of the components of the total statement. Their procedure was to look at where the group was now, to decide where they wanted to be and when, and to decide how to get there. Their membership was drawn from all functions and all levels of the business, and their work was co-ordinated at board level.

The mission statement reads as follows:

'We will be the leading country wide speciality store, the first choice for fashion and home furnishings for middle- and upper-income customers, characterized by our:

visual excitement and easy-to-shop environment
fashion authority
dominance in the most wanted merchandise categories
above-average quality and value for money
merchandise organized by end use, activity or emerging trend
customer dedication

We will produce above-average profits for department stores to meet group financial objectives.

We will develop an organizational environment which will attract, retain, develop and motivate high-calibre staff, dedicated to the implementing of our mission.'

The mission statement was promulgated throughout the company in every possible way, including a video interview with Ralph Halpern. But, of course, words are not enough. For the mission statement to mean anything, there must be action. In some ways this was easily done, because the effect of the statement was to create a revolution in the way Debenhams had done business.

From now on, it was intended to sell within the stores by end use. So, for example, instead of table cloths being sold in the linen department, they would be sold in that part of the store devoted to dining rooms. Likewise, tea towels would be sold in the kitchen section. Similarly, skirts had been sold in twenty-three different departments; these were reduced to five areas, like fashion-active, businesswear, everydaywear and so on.

The revolution in display was clear enough in principle, though the work involved in putting it into practice was immense. The implications for training were equally daunting. Staff would be involved in selling a range of products, many of which they had never in their life sold before: to be effective, they would need to be sufficiently expert to earn the customers' confidence. Debenhams response was to plan a major training programme, to begin in February 1987. This was initially based in one of the London stores and consisted of three weeks' off-the-job training for selected management teams, who were taken in over a period of time to ensure adequate staffing. Departmental managers would be brought in for the parts of the training relevant to their needs. Subsequent initial training would be given by those managers who had been through this programme.

Staff in Debenhams stores had been immediately transferred to a new bonus scheme, which could give up to 25 or 30 per cent of salary if targets were exceeded. Stores management was assessed on profitability and departmental management on sales. Bonus was awarded on a team basis and was seen as more of an incentive than the discretionary bonus that used to be awarded.

Burton had succeeded because it was clear about its business mission, and because it was generous in rewarding success. It set plans that were challenging but achievable, and it worked hard to master the business of change. It has set out to apply the same formula to Debenhams. It believes that in this way it will create commitment and a profitable and secure future.

10
Confidence in management: dedication

'Faced with the question of how to improve their competitiveness, a dozen heads of business would, more than likely, provide a dozen different answers. But whatever their preferred solution, the fact is that there would be no hope of success unless the management team was wholeheartedly committed to its objective,' wrote John Egan, the Chairman of Jaguar, in his contribution to the BIM report *Improving Management Performance.*

If top management is not committed, success is unlikely. But there are companies where management goes through the motions in all areas of endeavour, including creating commitment. For example, in one company we know there was a quality problem which management decided to try and tackle by establishing quality circles. They appointed a co-ordinator at senior middle-management level and left him to get on with it. In practice, they did not give their full support and were even unwilling to attend his introductory meetings. The lack of top-level commitment soon became obvious to the workforce and the programme died away.

What is impressive about the companies in our case studies is the way top management has been prepared to put itself 'on the line'. In one case after another, top management has developed a coherent business strategy and has been tenacious in ensuring that the workforce understand and are committed to it. The overall approach can be summed up in the phrase 'faith in people'.

Thus in Building Design Partnership, Professor Sir George Grenfell Baines and a few colleagues had a compelling belief that architects and other building professionals should be able to work as equal partners. They were ahead of their time, but despite many difficulties and setbacks they persisted; today the partnership is multidiscipline and flourishing.

Pilkington, in setting up the new Greengate plant, established the aims for the organization of the factory into a series of eight points which came to be called the 'organization philosophy'. It covered such matters as single status, accountability, overtime and so on. Management spent two years communicating the philosophy to anyone who would listen. The unions believed that management was moving too quickly, but management were convinced this was not the case. It pushed its beliefs and they were eventually accepted by the unions, together with the need to reform the negotiating structure to accommodate the new approach.

Rothmans developed principles of group working, based on the philosophy that the basic organizational unit should be the primary work group. So successful were these that it was decided to use the approach in their other factories. Putting the belief into practice was expensive. For example, at one of their older factories, practically every machine had to be moved.

Hardy Spicer is another example of a company whose management publicly committed itself to a new way forward. They demonstrated considerable courage, at a time of deep recession, in transferring out of the company some 45 per cent of its turnover in the form of propeller shafts. The reason was that they saw no long-term future in the shafts market, which was declining. They further committed themselves to signing long-term contracts which offered reductions in price in real terms. They met the challenge not only by investing in new machinery but by undertaking a major workforce retraining programme costing some 2 per cent of turnover.

The good companies have not only developed a philosophy of commitment but have been consistent with it over a long period of time. CMG has long been known for its open style of management. Burton has systematically developed its business goals and had a well-developed and generous bonus system. Perkin Elmer has worked hard over a number of years at its gain–sharing scheme. None could be accused of creating cynicism in their staff by following blindly every passing management fashion.

Creating commitment is hard. It is time-consuming, and the path is not always smooth. Managers who wish to create commitment need to be dedicated. Because of the effort they will need to make, they also need to be sure of their ground: to have clarified their attitudes to the workforce, and in particular to subjects like disclosure of information, involvement, sharing in success and accountability.

For example, not all managers believe in full disclosure of information to the workforce. Indeed, it is common to meet managers who take the view that the workforce will not understand information and that time spent in systematic disclosure is wasted. There are managers who take the view that bad news should not be disclosed in case it demoralizes the workforce, and that good news should be hidden in case the workforce wants to share in the benefits. There are managers who have tried to disclose information but have been discouraged.

Managers need to be dedicated to the idea of creating commitment if they are going to succeed. They need this dedication if only because of the amount of time required. We can see this clearly by looking at information disclosure and involvement. Disclosing information by means of briefing groups requires that time be put aside on a regular basis. In a busy business, this is not always easy to do, and the briefings can pass by default. Similarly, if, as can frequently happen, the workforce is not immediately impressed by the information being communicated, or does not understand it, time is required to repeat and simplify the message.

Likewise with involvement. The whole process requires time. To some managers it may seem easier to develop the ideal blueprint for the business without contributions from the workforce. In times of crisis there is perhaps no other alternative. But apart from those rare crises, managers who want to involve their workforce will have to listen carefully to the thoughts and ideas presented to them. They will need to consider them in good faith and be prepared to accept those ideas which happen to be better than their own, and to explain fully why some ideas which seem satisfactory to the workforce are not acceptable.

The manager who sets out to create commitment by delegating responsibility down the line finds that he needs to exercise self-discipline. He must resist the temptation to interfere. What is more difficult, he finds that he is not fully aware of every detail of what is happening in his department. For delegation to work, there needs to be a clear understanding on such matters between a manager and his boss.

Managers who do not believe in disclosure and involvement are unlikely to start along the path we have charted for creating commitment. Likewise, managers who are temperamentally attracted to disclosure and involvement need to be sure that all their effort will achieve results. The problem they face is that commitment, if it has been absent, cannot be turned on like a tap. Managers need to work at it, and the results appear only slowly.

If creating commitment requires vision and effort, maintaining commitment requires time and constant attention. If management attention wanders, workforce commitment can be at risk. We saw this at Raleigh where, as the result of a reorganization, the Lightweight bike workforce lost its sense of team spirit, and morale deteriorated. Fortunately, management saw what was happening and the situation was restored.

Maintaining commitment requires an approach of dedicated professionalism. It requires that top managers understand their business and are prepared to think about business goals. It means they need to be clear about the nature of commitment and how it should be created.

This discipline requires that they plan their work in a way that allows for adequate time to brief people; that they will be active in seeking the involvement of their staff and ready to take on board their contribution; that they systematically practice delegation and ensure that their staff become accountable for their own work; that they are jealous of management integrity and ensure that nothing is done that will damage trust; and that they ensure a fair distribution of rewards.

Management can reinforce their professionalism by ensuring that there are no unnecessary management overheads such as an over-large headquarters staff or too many levels of management. In our case studies there has often been severe pruning at headquarters and a sharp reduction in the levels of management.

The practice of commitment may seem like a counsel of perfection, ideal in theory but unattainable in practice. The reality is that there are companies, including those in our case studies, who have embraced the practice and been successful. Commitment requires effort, but it can be done and is worthwhile.

Case 13: Hardy Spicer

Hardy Spicer, manufacturer of car transmission systems, is a company within the Universal Transmission Division of the giant GKN Group. In the late seventies, Hardy Spicer, along with much of the Midlands engineering industry, faced the traumatic consequences of increased competition and economic depression. Its costs were out of line, particularly in contrast to those of its Japanese competitors. It was heavily overmanned and its quality was variable. Today, it is successful, profitable and, as far as this is ever possible, has an assured future.

How did it get there? The answer is threefold. First, like so many other companies, it faced up to the problem of overmanning and ineffective working. It declared major redundancies and changed working practices. Second, it got to grips with its markets, its suppliers and its manufacturing. It set out to generate commitment by increasing management competence. Finally, it has undertaken a major reinvestment programme. The first test was in the marketplace. For many years, the power transmission in a motor-driven vehicle was via a propeller shaft to the rear wheels. Today many cars, particularly the smaller compact cars, are driven from the engine to the front wheels via constant velocity or CV joints, or by a propeller shaft to independent rear suspension units incorporating CV joints.

The industry has divided itself internationally. Most European and Eastern cars are compact and front wheel driven. The USA still produces predominantly large cars, rear wheel driven, though this is changing fast.

The suppliers of CV joints were protected by patent designs for many years, and because of the changeover from propeller to CV joints, the industry, despite the decline in world production of cars, retained its buoyancy internationally. (In the UK, the number of cars produced has, of course, continued to decline.)

At the end of the seventies, some 45 per cent of Hardy Spicer's turnover was in propeller shafts, and profitability was in decline, despite good income from royalties. Quality was inconsistent, and prices were higher than in Europe and considerably higher than in Japan. There was excess production capacity within the industry, and the car manufacturers were themselves becoming increasingly interested in the manufacture of CV joints.

The board decided to take a hard look at its future. As a first step, to ensure fresh thinking, changes were made in senior management. The second was to take a close look at profitability. This confirmed weaknesses in propeller shafts. These were in the tertiary stage of their product life cycle, and volumes were reducing rapidly. The market was expected to shrink further. The CV joints market was growing. If Hardy Spicer were to compete successfully in this market, it would need to reduce costs and prices. The review thus produced three major decisions:

(i)   to rationalize the product
(ii)   to reduce prices to obtain volume
(iii) to reduce costs to maintain profitability.

The rationalization that resulted from the review was quite dramatic. The company simply decided to stop making car and small commercial shafts, and transferred production to another part of the GKN group. Heavy shafts were retained on an interim basis. Management decided to stake its future on the CV joint. In effect, the company rationalized by giving away half its turnover and by staking its future on the other half – a clear display of management courage.

The second aspect of policy was to cut prices to obtain volume. So competitive was the market that the only choice was to negotiate long-term contracts with significant price advantages for volume business. In the case of BL, the company aimed for a sole-supplier agreement. Such an agreement would allow for greater stability and the confidence to make longer-term planning decisions. The agreement was obtained, but the price was high – a commitment to reduce prices in real terms every year.

The third aim, cost reduction, followed clearly from the second. Productivity had to improve substantially, and this was to be achieved by a variety of means: labour costs had to be reduced, organization had to be improved, material specifications had to be tightened, and quality had to be built into the process.

The reduction in labour costs was accomplished in two ways. There was the sad, sorry process of redundancies and factory closures. In 1979, the company had three factories: the main factory in Birmingham and a feeder factory there; and another feeder factory in the North-East. By 1983, both feeder factories had been closed and there had been a major reduction in Birmingham. Altogether, a quarter of the labour force was made redundant.

The redundancies were made on the principle of eliminating all jobs not essential to the survival of the business: the 'nice to have' jobs were to go. Particular emphasis was placed on the indirects and the staff. Management also took a firm line on selection for redundancy: the 'non-committed' and the 'It can't be done' brigade were encouraged to go. So, rather sadly, were the less able. The redundancies were a mixture of voluntary and forced.

Management then set out to ensure that communications were improved and the remaining workforce used more effectively. On the production side, one tier of management, the superintendent level, was eliminated; the manager's span of control was reduced by increasing their numbers from three to five, giving them a chance to operate more positively across a smaller area. Without the superintendents, the managers had direct contact with their foremen, who had been much criticized for not doing a foreman's job. Greater responsibility was given to the foremen, who were also made accountable. A number could not withstand the change and became casualties, some returning to their natural roles of setters. Some new, younger, engineering-trained foremen took their place.

In addition, the quality department was substantially reduced in size and responsibility. The 150 inspectors were replaced with 30 quality engineers, responsible to the production foremen.

Operators became responsible for their own quality, with production foremen becoming accountable. Quality engineers were appointed, not to inspect, but to quality-audit processes and machines. Scrap levels eventually fell, and productivity increased accordingly. Further moves have taken place since, further reducing inspectors and eliminating all quality foremen.

There was a subtle change of emphasis. As Managing Director David Mackin explained, 'The function of the quality inspectors used to be to prevent the operators producing bad work. Operators who *had* produced bad work could always blame the quality inspector. They could ask why the inspector had not prevented the bad work . . . Now, the function of the quality engineer is to help the operator produce good work. The operator has the responsibility for quality, and if he has problems, he can call on the engineer to help him'.

Productivity improved because management improved. Wasted time was reduced by better planning, fewer set-ups, more consistent production runs: More jobs were made right first time, thus reducing scrap and rework. Each operator became more effective without having to work any harder.

When the upturn in business came at the end of 1982, the company was able to take advantage. More pieces were being produced in 1982 than in 1979, with 40 per cent less people being employed.

These changes were not imposed by management. They were achieved by careful but firm negotiation. The company made a conscious attempt to remain in contact with its employees. There were regular Joint Industrial Council meetings to discuss all changes, including detailed changes. Such was the pace, however, that the change in attitudes had to be accomplished by firm leadership. There was no time for formal retraining. People just had to get on with the job.

The reduced span of control obviously helped here, as did the atmosphere of high unemployment and depression in the area. The unions and their members were questioning, but they were aware that real threats could totally put the company out of business. The real burden fell on management. Many of them were new to their jobs, but it was they who had to communicate the important new message.

Hardy Spicer benefited from the effect increased international competition was having on its suppliers. It became possible to impose tighter specifications, which meant less machining and higher rates of conversion. This was important, since materials counted for 45 per cent of the cost of manufacture. The company became closer to fewer more reliable quality producers. Often the initial prices that had to be paid were higher, but these higher costs were easily recovered in improved manufacturing performance. The men were actually able to get on with the job. They were not forever reworking substandard materials, or having to keep changing jobs because the raw products supplied were not up to scratch. The men felt happier because of this, and found it easier to stay committed.

Similarly, Hardy Spicer increased its emphasis on designing products for ease of manufacture. Parts were standardized. The resultant higher volumes and reduced variety created greater machine utilization and less work in progress. Detailed design changes to eliminate difficult and expensive manufacturing operations reduced costs without weakening the product. Again, the men were able to get on with the job.

The company used to employ a piecework bonus scheme for direct operators. Traditionally such schemes have been divisive and have not always stimulated output. In effect, they have been used to guarantee a fairly fixed take-home pay. In 1979, in response to this, the company had introduced a factory-wide productivity bonus. Since then, bonus earnings have increased steadily. Interestingly enough, the individual piecework element has been retained, but is less significant than the company bonus. Because the bonus has been increasing, there has been little problem in restricting base take-home pay.

By 1983, the immediate crisis was over. There was a rising demand for the product, and output had risen in 1983 by 20 per cent, with no increase in direct labour. The number of direct operators was, in fact, continuing to fall, but their hours of work were increasing to compensate. Indirect and staff numbers were falling faster, and their hours were not compensated.

The question the company now faced was this: could it maintain commitment and output now that the relatively 'good' times had returned? It had to do so against a future in which there was going to be major reinvestment, with more automation of manufacture and reduction of work handling; more computer-aided design and engineering systems; and a need for more demanding and new skills.

The answer was found not only in increased management competence but in the growing maturity of the workforce. An example of this was when the time came for the company to introduce three-shift working.

Although seen as necessary by the workforce, this was not popular. In the bad old days, the workforce might have dug in their heels. On this occasion, the approach was positive. The workers agreed but asked to make their own arrangements to meet the manning requirements. They came back to the company with a planned distribution of work which suited their own needs and met the company's.

But the full flowering of workforce maturity was seen when the company decided to make its major investment in new equipment. The project the company unfolded was indeed exciting. It was to set up a 'greenfield' site – on space cleared within the factory – and to install equipment as modern as any in the world. The machinery, like so much modern equipment, was impressive. Not only did it work to incredible tolerances – within one-thirtieth of the thickness of a human hair – but it monitored its own performance, corrected its own faults and kept an eye on its own maintenance. Its continued accuracy was such that, although it made components in tens of millions, the few faulty components that slipped through were numbered in the low hundreds and were getting fewer all the time.

Manning levels, of course, had to be substantially reduced. The old equipment required 40 people per shift, and produced 240 units per hour, from which 30 per cent would be rejected as substandard. The new equipment would require 7 or 8 people to produce the same number per hour, and less than 1 per cent would be rejected.

The new equipment and low manning placed all sorts of demands on the workforce. For example, work like cleaning used to be undertaken by internal staff but was now handled by contractors. The absence of internal cleaning staff meant that oil spillages and suchlike would frequently have to be dealt with by the firm's new technology team. They were prepared to do it but, not unexpectedly, they were not prepared to make a meal out of such unwelcome tasks. The old sawdust-bucket routine was pensioned off and replaced with something quicker and more efficient.

The new sophisticated machinery also required a technically sophisticated workforce. The Hardy Spicer workforce was not by any stretch of the imagination unskilled, but it did not match up to the new skills required. The challenge was how to recruit those new skills. Should the company look outside, or should it upgrade those who worked for it already?

In opting to train from within its own workforce, the company had three considerations in mind. The first was that it had a duty to provide opportunities to those who had worked so loyally during the difficult times in the late seventies and early eighties. The second was that it knew its workforce and what it was capable of, and there was no doubt it would rise to the challenge. The third and final point was that the company was now operating in an environment in which the only long-term solution was to train its own workforce.

The days were now gone when skilled men could be recruited from myriad little companies that made up the industrial scene in Birmingham. There were now very few such companies. Economic recession had seen to that. Nor was there an assured flow of the young and technically-skilled from the machine-tool companies.

Those companies had been decimated. Realistically, companies now have to provide their own training.

So the company decided to meet the new challenge with its own workforce. To do so, it had to embark on an extensive and very expensive course of retraining. It therefore had to be sure of the abilities and commitment of those who were to be retrained.

If the company had ever had any doubts about the response of the workforce, it was soon disabused. For the forty training places on offer, there were 800 internal applicants. That was out of a total workforce of just over 2,000. Selection was by a written examination whose purpose was to establish not so much existing skills as the capacity for being trained.

What was on offer was a six-months multiskilling course which would include electrics, electronics, induction hardening, metallurgy, metrology, the basics of statistical process control, and so on. The training would start at a more elementary level and would then become more specialized. Those who acquired specialized skills would later have a responsibility to train others.

Training would take place in company lecture rooms, at the local technical college and on suppliers' premises. The 'students' were in fact flown around Europe to be trained by suppliers on how to use and maintain the new equipment, which was installed with their help. Thirty-nine out of the forty completed the course, and now another forty are being trained.

Interestingly enough, those who took part in the training were not paid overtime and actually suffered a reduction in pay. This was fully explained before the studies commenced, and had the merit of ensuring that the students were motivated not by money but by a desire to improve their skills. Not that training saved the company any money. Its cost amounted to £1,500,000 out of a turnover of £70,000,000 — about 2 per cent.

To mark the division between the old and the new, it was decided that the greenfield site would be fenced off from the rest of the factory. The new layout is much more of a continuous flow type of operation, and there are visibly fewer people. In time, all production will use such new equipment. The age profile of the workforce is such that any job losses will occur in due course by natural wastage.

Hardy Spicer has been through troubled times. It has had to turn its working practices on its head. It has lost staff, and those who have remained have had to show flexibility and a willingness to learn new skills. It has suffered great traumas, but with visibly better management and an undoubtedly committed workforce, its future should be assured.

11
Confidence in management: competence

Workforce commitment and management incompetence cannot coexist. If management does not know what it wants to do, or how to do it, then the workforce cannot know to what it should be committed. If management chops and changes for no apparent reason and fails to plan where planning would make a difference, then the workforce is more likely to be cynical than committed. Only competent managers enjoy committed workforces.

To be competent does not mean to be always right. That is scarcely possible in a complex and rapidly changing world: too much is unpredictable. In such conditions, being always right means not taking any risks. No business can survive without taking risks. Being competent also does not mean having full information about the technical aspects of the business. The pace of technical development is now so fast that even the specialists have difficulty in keeping up.

Competence means establishing and communicating a sense of direction and harnessing and developing the appropriate organizational skills to achieve the optimum business results. It requires an intense sensitivity to the market and a fine appreciation of what the organization has to offer. It starts by looking outwards for opportunity and inwards for resources.

The Burton Group is an example of an organization that has developed and communicated a clear sense of direction. In the mid-seventies, it did not know where it was going. Much of its strength was based on a section of the market, made-to-measure, that was in decline. It had diversified into a variety of businesses, including business stationery through Rymans and cameras and hi-fi through Greens.

Ralph Halpern and his team focussed the group's attention. Its mission was to be the fashion retailing expert of the 1980s. The peripheral businesses did not fit this concept and were sold. Burton had to accept that their shops, ranging from 1,000 to 3,000 square feet, were too small to offer a wide range to everybody. It decided the shops should each concentrate on a segment of the market; Top Man on men between 15 and 24 and so on.

The Building Design Partnership set out to create a multidiscipline practice in an industry where the different professionals are traditionally not integrated. How they did so is told in the case study at the end of this chapter. The formal expression of their philosophy was set out in three goals, known colloquially as 'the three Qs'.

These goals — quality of product, quality of service and quality of life — recognized the idealistic desire to achieve artistic and technical excellence, the commercial need to sustain a high reputation and the aspiration to contribute to society.

What is particularly interesting is the third goal, quality of life, which was an internal goal recognizing the needs of the differing professions for autonomy. This formal recognition of the need to respect the aspirations of the different professional groups provided the framework which made multidiscipline working possible.

Goals are difficult to establish. They need to be credible, achievable and able to stand the test of time. They have to be examined to ensure they reflect the organization's philosophy and that they will provide answers to hard questions. If they are not adequate and management disregard them, they will fall into disuse. Establishing worthwhile goals requires considerable management attention.

When Ralph Halpern took over at Burton in the mid-seventies, he and his board set out to meet the group management around the country. He asked them to describe what they felt was wrong and what needed to be done. The board reported back fully to a management conference some six months later. They gave the managers their findings exactly as they had been reported to them, and then set out the board's view of the company mission. The mission statement was a board responsibility, though informed by the views of the managers. The managers could see how it had been developed and its communication was effective. They in turn knew what to report to their staff.

There are other organizations which have used large-scale employee opinion surveys as the basis for establishing organizational goals. The danger with that approach is that the process can take a long time and leave employees with the impression that management cannot make up its mind.

In all cases, the full benefit of goals is achieved only when they form the basis for more local objectives. A board's goal of market penetration becomes the sales manager's objective of establishing an overseas sales office within the year. The maintenance department's goal of a trouble-free operation becomes the objective of ensuring all repairs are correctly effected within twenty-four hours. Likewise a company goal — like the Debenhams goal of attracting, retaining, developing and motivating high-calibre staff — can provide excellent guidelines for the personnel and training departments.

However, establishing objectives from goals is not always easy. When Burton took over Debenhams and established new goals for that company, it set up a dozen task forces and a major training programme to put them into effect. Schweppes established as a company goal that it would become the lowest-cost supplier of branded soft drinks in the UK. It put this into effect through a 'best practice' policy, which meant a management commitment to gathering information on costs throughout the world, and applying the results to its own operations.

Goals need to be challenging and to make people feel significant. Jaguar sets a quality goal of 'right first time'. Such goals appeal to people's inherent competitiveness. They like to think they have worthwhile goals to achieve and standards to maintain, feeling the part they play is significant.

Goals set a direction for an organization. They show it how to react to the change and flux of external pressures. They do not abolish those pressures. Managers are still obliged to cope with uncertainty. Their competence is challenged and they have every opportunity to make mistakes. How their mistakes are handled can influence the degree of commitment of the workforce.

An atmosphere of continual botched opportunities and constant changes of plan can destroy commitment — especially if it really is due to incompetence. Where uncertainty is inherent, a function of the unpredictability of markets, fluctuations of currency or the actions of foreign governments, managers best maintain commitment by ensuring that the workforce is given the fullest possible explanation of events: at least they can point to what the company is trying to achieve, and the difficulties in the way of attainment.

Case 14: Building Design Partnership

Professional staff have an inherent desire for autonomy. Their natural state is to be sole practitioners responsible for their own judgements. They do not like to be managed. It is an attitude difficult to maintain in the face of factors like the inexorable growth of knowledge and the increasing complexity of human affairs, not to mention intense competitive pressures.

Among professionals, architects have a particular problem. Their sense of autonomy is allied to a strong creative drive. But unlike artists, they cannot work alone with malleable materials. Their canvas is the client's brief and can frequently be of hideous complexity. Their materials include not only physical things but the raw skills of countless other professionals. Architects aspire to harness them all. Their buildings reflect the integration they have been able to achieve.

Integrating the efforts of other professionals is difficult. Their training is different. They claim a greater expertise in their particular area. Such professions have had (and still have) a tendency to fragment. Engineers have split into civil, structural, mechanical, electrical, control, heating and ventilating and many more; surveyors into building, land, mineral rights, quantity, estate agency and so on.

There are differences in style. Architects generally prefer to work in small groups. Engineers measure their status by the number of people they control. Graphic artists are said to regard people over 40 as in their dotage, while rumour has it that civil engineers regard anybody under 40 as 'unsafe'.

More ominously for the architect, the new professions nibble away at what architects regarded as 'their' market. Interior designers have laid successful claim to the inside of buildings. Building surveyors lay claim to the refurbishment of existing buildings and indeed sometimes state that they have replaced architects. In fact, of course, architects do have significant interior design work and do refurbish many existing buildings. But the competition is intense, and they can lay no proprietary right to this work.

How the problem of integration is tackled varies. Some large organizations buy all the skills they require in-house. Others co-ordinate the various contractors and subcontractors themselves. Architectural practices habitually offer to co-ordinate the other professionals. There are a very few practices which set out to establish an equal partnership between members of different professions. To be successful in so doing requires sufficient scale and momentum to sustain balanced resources in all the key disciplines. One such practice is Building Design Partnership, established in 1961. It was at that time a brand new concept in the world of building.

Today it employs nearly 1,100 people in eight offices throughout the United Kingdom, of which 290 are architects, just over 100 are civil and structural engineers and about 100 mechanical engineers; 60 electrical engineers; 40 or so are in project management and project planning; 80 in quantity surveying, and 20 or so in each of landscape design, interior and industrial design, public-health engineering, graphics/models, and computing; and about 10 in planning. The firm is truly multidiscipline.

Its clients are corporate, commercial and public, and its commissions have included the Halifax Building Society Headquarters, Ealing town centre and the Queen's Medical Centre, Nottingham. One of its proudest commissions is the design of the UK terminal for the Channel Tunnel. Its creativity as an organization is recognized by the many competitions it wins and the many awards it receives, including thirty Civic Trust Awards.

How has BDP so successfully integrated the efforts of such a diverse range of specialists? It would be nice to be able to give a straightforward answer, but the truth is the firm has evolved over the years. What it does today is a direct result of much experience and thought. The initial impetus came from Professor Sir George Grenfell Baines. The inspiration for his vision was the seminal ideas generated by the Bauhaus school in the 1930s in Germany, which attempted to create a unity of arts and technology by bringing together artists, sculptors, industrial designers, photographers and architects.

But the road was long and hard. The war, in his case, catalysed both expansion and group working. But after the war things changed. In Baines' words, 'The momentum of our war effort carried with it the group ideal and steadied any wavering tendencies. But ever since the war ended, the changing state of society seems to have affected us'. He went on to say that the major problem was the maintenance of a common working policy. A further problem was the 'personal' client, which could effectively distract attention from the needs of the group.

In any case, Baines' group lost its momentum. In 1950 he reorganized, setting up a series of five self-contained firms in Preston

and elsewhere in the North of England. Each of these firms contributed towards a common research fund. Effectively, the 'collective
experiment had led back to individual independence', though with
the difference that there was a form of central association. In the
late 1950s, one of the member firms, Grenfell Baines and Har-
greaves, started to recruit engineers, and the first non-architect, a
quantity surveyor, was made a full partner in 1959. Taking a non-
architect into partnership was a major step forward at that time.

It was not until 1961 that Baines and his colleagues set up what
has become today's Building Design Partnership. It has succeeded
and prospered. Its success rested initially on the continuing vision of
its founders, tempered as it was by experience. Its continuation lies
in its ability to transmit that vision to those who now work for it. The
formal expression of its philosophy is found in its attention to goals,
its ability to balance democracy and authority, together with its
ideas about process, and its sharing of rewards.

The firm's goals, known colloquially as 'the three Qs', are:

(i)   quality of product – a better environment
(ii)   quality of service to client and community
(iii) quality of life for ourselves in doing it.

It is unusual to see such a clear hierarchy of goals. The first reflects
the idealistic desire to achieve artistic and technical excellence.
The second expresses both the commercial need to sustain a high
reputation and the aspiration to contribute to society. The third is
an internal goal. It reflects in this case the professionals' need for
autonomy, creativity and adequate income. BDP aim to achieve it
by balancing what is known in the firm as 'the three Rs': recognition,
responsibility and reward.

How are these goals expressed in organizational terms? The
answer is found in a fusion of democracy and matrix management.
The chairman and chief executive are elected by all the sixty plus
partners every two years. The chief executive nominates the senior
management.

Previously, when it was first decided not to involve all partners in
all decisions, all the senior management had been elected. It was
felt, however, that the best were not always elected, and that
seniority of service and personality were sometimes given undue
emphasis. The partners therefore voted to change the system, and
powers of appointment were vested in the chief executive.

The work of the practice is, of course, project-based. Projects are handled through offices and draw on the range of functional skills needed. The resulting organization has to accommodate the pressures of developing the business, working to the quality required and completing on time and to budget. The tension is handled within a matrix which has five office executives – who can come from any profession – with line responsibilities on the one axis; four profession chairmen with quality, training and professional responsibilities on the other, together with two central executive partners. One of these, the business partner, has administrative and financial responsibilities. The other, the practice partner, has responsibilities for the future development of the practice, marketing and quality of work.

The business partner meets on a regular basis with the office executives, and the practice partner with the profession chairmen. The two executive partners and the chief executive form a central executive group which meets formally every two weeks. This formal structure, based on consent, provides the framework for a great deal of discussion and ferment and a continuous attempt to reach consensus.

The organization could be described as 'free form', designed to allow the maximum opportunity for creativity and autonomy but with a sufficient framework to ensure business effectiveness and regular attention to the organization's goals.

Its chairman, Keith Scott, feels that BDP is at its best when it works as a unified design team. This will only work, he feels 'with the conviction that ours is the right way to produce the buildings that society needs, and when there is an underlying respect for the quality and uniqueness of contribution of each profession – whether it be responsible for a regional structure plan or for the pattern of tiles in a food court'. Without those convictions, so-called multidiscipline practices 'disintegrate at the first sign of trouble'. He points out that tension in a design session can rise to breaking point yet the high point of tension has frequently been the breakthrough to new levels of excellence.

What the approach means in practice is that both project and profession partners have a legitimate input into each project. This creates a tremendous tension out of which comes a constant day-to-day interaction between the needs of the project and the requirements and objectives of the professions working on it.

Such tension could, of course, destroy commitment and create antipathy. The mediocre could easily supplant the superb. The firm handles this by having a very carefully structured process by which each project is organized, monitored and controlled. This is the point at which creativity has free reign and meets face to face with the realities of the marketplace.

So each project is analysed and a tailor-made framework established at the beginning. Obviously, there are some common factors to each project, but there are also some peculiar to certain projects. The process has to be flexible enough to suit the individual architect and design team – and, of course, be acceptable to the client.

There is thus no standard set of bureaucratic rules. This, in the view of Richard Saxon, practice partner at the time of writing, is the secret of organizing professionals; it is established very clearly with the client at the proposal stage. From it follows the need to define objectives, to set up a plan of work and to discuss with each of the profession leaders how they are going to relate, at what point they are going to come in with their services, how long it will take, when their contribution can be appraised, and when overall quality can be appraised.

There is often a formal post-project analysis in which the contributors look at the total effort in terms of how they did on that job. Was the client kept happy? Will he come back with more business? Is the project one to be proud of? What, if anything, went wrong? What went right? Could it, with hindsight, have been done better? Is there anything reusable for other projects? What are the lessons to be learned?

The firm consciously looks at where they have been, because that way there is a better chance of doing better next time. The whole process, of course, serves the additional purpose of allowing those participating in the project to gain recognition for their contribution, and to savour the sense of achievement that comes from a job well done. It also gives them the opportunity to see how they might improve in the future and thus plays a major part in building commitment.

Within that framework, particular attention is paid to communications. In practice, in such a widely dispersed firm with so many projects under-way at any one time, and with so many people out of the office, communications are bound to be difficult. BDP tackles this in formal and informal ways. People are always free to talk to each other: intense communication is encouraged across all levels, and there are no hierarchical rules.

Formally, at most locations, there is an office meeting once a month. Part of that meeting is on a seminar basis, where people are given the opportunity to describe projects that have been completed and the successes and failures. People are given the chance to boast, and the partnership learns about successful solutions and avoids having to reinvent the wheel. There is also an in-house magazine which goes around the firm and is written so that it can be circulated to clients. It is used for describing aspects of projects that people have found interesting.

The firm aims to provide responsibility, recognition and reward. It sets out to achieve this by a regular system of appraisal, which is applied to all (including partners). It is worth mentioning that although appraisal is commonplace in industry, it is less common in the professions. For example, straw polls at meetings of solicitors suggest that only about one in ten are subject to some form of formal appraisal; it is also a fair judgement that the bulk of the medical profession in the UK is resistant to formal appraisal. At BDP appraisal is regular and thorough, and both profession managers and appropriate project managers are consulted.

The qualities assessed include, amongst others, creativity, identification, leadership, reputation, negotiating skills, decision-making, anticipation, programmes, budgets and communications. There is one section on the appraisal form labelled 'expediency'. This recognizes that such factors as market demand can have an effect on salary, and that people sometimes need to be paid more for their skills than their contribution would strictly demand.

The appraisal is used to assess how the partnership's total predicted income should be shared. Partners and employees are awarded income shares under the various appraisal headings. The shares awarded are totalled for the whole firm and divided into the sum available. This gives a value to each income share and

$$salary = shares\ awarded \times income\ value\ of\ income\ shares.$$

So if somebody is awarded one hundred shares and the value of each share is £130, his or her salary will be £13,000 for the ensuing year.

Of course partners are not salaried, even though their drawings are based on income share allocations. What they receive under the scheme is effectively 'payment on account' or an advance on their share in the profits. A partners' share assessment is made by the chairman and chief executive.

Partners are placed in one of ten bands, and their position is reassessed by the chairman and chief executive every two to three years. The partners know each others' salaries. They also have the opportunity to nominate their own band and discuss their views with the chief executive and chairman.

BDP then goes on to give staff an opportunity to contribute to the internal funding of the firm and to share in the profit generated after payment of salaries and expenses. The scheme applies to all, whatever their status, who have two years' service or more. How does it work? Basically, the firm's requirement for internal capital funding is expressed in what are called 'funding units'. The value of each of these units at the time of writing is £25.

Ordinary staff may purchase one funding unit for every income share they hold. Thus, somebody holding 100 income shares may contribute up to £2,500. Those at associate grade may, if they choose, contribute up to one and a half times their income shares entitlement. Those who volunteer to contribute must take up a minimum of 10 per cent of their entitlement. All are given three years to pay.

Members other than equity partners can, if they take up their full entitlement, contribute up to 48 per cent of the internal capital funding. The equity partners have to hold the majority and must contribute the balance of capital required when full entitlements have not been taken up.

The return on the funding subscribed is made in two ways. The first is guaranteed and is paid whether or not BDP makes a profit. The amount paid is related to BDP's borrowing rate. It is, in effect, an interest payment. The second is related to BDP's profit after all salary, expenses and interest payments have been made.

Holding the funding units is worthwhile: currently the people below partner level have contributed 40 per cent of the internal capital funding. All payments are accompanied by a certificate from the firm's auditors.

The keys to BDP's success have included a willingness to articulate its goals; to value the views of each of the professions and to ensure that all have the opportunity to contribute equally; to provide systematically for the sharing of rewards and for the opportunity to contribute to the firm's working capital; and to create and maintain an organization designed to recognize and utilize the tensions inherent in multi-profession working.

Integrating professional workers is not easy. Anybody who has worked in the Health Service will confirm this. So will anybody involved in examining the possibility that solicitors might form practices with other professionals. BDP has succeeded in integrating professionals, and in an area where integration is notoriously difficult. What has been achieved should not be underestimated.

12
US experience with workforce commitment

Traditionally the USA is the home of the rugged individualist and the birthplace of scientific management. Labour/management strife has a long and bloody tradition, with union-busting almost a national pastime. Paradoxically, however, it is also the home of Hewlett-Packard, Johnson and Johnson, IBM and 3M, to name but a few of the stars of *In Search of Excellence* — highly successful companies which have strong corporate cultures, emphasizing the importance of people, vision, values and commitment.

In Search of Excellence, and its sequel *A Passion for Excellence*, look at the trail-blazers of US business and attribute a large part of their success to the importance they give to people. 'Productivity through people' is one of the eight keys to excellence, closely followed by 'Hands on, Value driven' (or, in simple terms: Get on with the job while always remembering the values of the company) — characterized by, among other things, MBWA (management by walking about), an acronym with an assured place in management jargon.

Great things have been achieved through the commitment of the people in those leading companies: IBM designed and launched their personal computer in 22 months; 25% of 3M's products did not exist five years ago; Johnson and Johnson survived the Tylanol poisoning threat by making their principles a reality and withdrawing the product nationwide at a cost of many hundreds of millions of dollars.

Perhaps most impressive of all, the employees of Delta Airlines clubbed together when the company faced a crisis and bought the company a complete $30 million aircraft — wrapped in red ribbon as it was rolled from the hanger.

Spectacular as they are, these examples come from an elite of companies. Perhaps there are special circumstances that account for them, or perhaps they are unique and quite untypical of the rest of American industry. There is increasing evidence that neither is the case.

Before looking at this more recent experience, however, it is worth exploring something of the development of participative management in the USA. Unless individually acknowledged, material in this chapter is based on published sources, including *Business Week, International Management* and *The Economist*.

Many observers take the famous Hawthorne experiments as the starting point. Indeed, the words 'Hawthorne effect' have entered the management vocabulary. Although deeply flawed as experiments, they were interpreted as evidence that human behavioural factors can influence output and productivity just as strongly as scientific control of the work process and working environment. More recent reinterpretation places emphasis on the fact that the workers were involved in decision-making to a large extent, both as to working methods and in the conduct of the experiment itself.

Study of the Hawthorne effect triggered a movement towards the application of behavioural science to management and organization. Pioneering work by behavioural scientists such as Lickert, Maslow, Argyris and Bennis led to the evolution of a new discipline — organizational development (OD). This concentrated on ways in which fundamental intervention at the organizational level could develop the organization and lead to improved performance.

In spite of the spread of OD, however, it was largely confined to managerial levels, with virtually no union involvement. It was regarded by many as a gimmick — derided by those who did not understand it as the 'happy people' programme. It was not until some time in the 1970s, when the unions began to be involved and the 'quality of working life' (QWL) approach evolved, that it began to have a major impact.

Quality of working life is a loose term used to describe a general approach to management and organization that covers every aspect of work. QWL attempts to identify changes that will add to the intrinsic meaning of work and enhance the quality of employees' working lives. It has also been defined as a process by which an organization attempts to unlock the potential of its people by involving them in decisions affecting their working lives.

General Motors, Tarrytown[*]

The history of General Motors Tarrytown plant can be taken as an illustration of the decisive changes that often took place in the 1970s. The plant would never have found itself in the mess it did if the lessons of Hawthorne had been absorbed and applied. On the other hand, it was the application of those lessons — in the 'quality of working life' (QWL) movement — that corrected the problem and led to recovery. In 1970, Tarrytown had one of the poorest labour relations and production records in General Motors. In seven years the plant had been turned around to become one of the better operations.

In the late 1960s and early 1970s, the Tarrytown plant suffered from high absenteeism and labour turnover. Operating costs were high. Frustration, fear and mistrust ruled. At times, there were upwards of 2,000 work grievances outstanding. Management was on the defensive, very secretive about forthcoming changes, using its authority to impose discipline and playing everything by the book. Employees saw their foremen as insensitive dictators and the company as an impersonal bureaucratic machine. Warnings, disciplinary layoffs and firings were commonplace.

In April 1971, Tarrytown was under threat and the assembly of trucks suspended. Two departments, Hard Trim and Soft Trim, were to be moved to a renovated area of the former truck line. The plant manager saw the need for change and also an opportunity. He suggested to some key union officials that, if they would co-operate, he would put pressure on his own management to adopt a QWL approach.

The suggestion was accepted and the new climate triggered a breakthrough. The planning of the move for the two trim departments was going on in the usual way through the industrial engineers and technical specialists. Two supervisors, however, sensing change, proposed that the workers be involved in planning the move. In spite of some scepticism, this was done. The result was an outpouring of ideas. Hundreds of suggestions were made, many of which were extremely valuable and quickly adopted. The move, when it came, was made with remarkably few grievances, and the plant easily made its production schedule deadlines. This success was repeated the following year with the involvement of the

[*]This account draws on the article by Robert H. Guest, 'Quality of Working Life — Learning from Tarrytown', *Harvard Business Review*, July/August 1979.

employees in the complete rearrangement of the Chassis Department.

At about this point, in 1973, the United Auto Workers' Union (UAW) and General Motors signed an historic national agreement. The contract contained a brief 'letter of agreement', signed by Irving Bluestone, vice-president of the GM department of UAW, and George Morris, head of industrial relations for GM. Both parties committed themselves to establishing formal mechanisms for exploring new ways of dealing with the quality of work life. This was the first time QWL was explicitly addressed in any major US labour–management contract.

The change in climate was reflected in a speech by Irving Blue-stone, repeated many times in various forms, and regarded by many as the kick-off speech for the QWL movement. In it, Bluestone reversed the usual sequence and called on management to co-operate with the workers, rather than the other way around. Co-operation should enhance human dignity, tap creative resources and involve workers in decision-making to develop a more satisfactory work-life.

The 1973 agreement 'legitimized' the local efforts at Tarrytown and gave them a boost. In April 1974, management and unions worked with a consultant to help break through the hostility and communications barriers. A series of problem-solving training sessions was set up on Saturdays, for eight hours each day. The sessions began in September 1974 with 34 volunteers from two shifts. Management agreed to pay for six hours of the training and the men volunteered their own time for the rest. The ideas generated by these sessions were impressive, and co-operation from the union was enthusiastic. Soon after the programme, workers began developing solutions to problems of water leaks, glass breakage and moulding damage.

In spite of the OPEC oil crisis which led to the shut-down of the second shift, with loss of 2,000 jobs, the movement built on its previous success in 1975. A programme of 27 hours of off-time instruction was devised. Of the 600 eligible employees, 570 volunteered to take part. Four trainers, two from the unions and two from management, were selected and trained to run the programme.

Unfortunately, progress with this programme was disrupted, after the first 60 participants had completed their sessions, by a return to two-shift operation. Capitalizing on the mutual trust that had been building up, however, management and the union agreed to set up an orientation programme for hundreds of newly hired employees. This programme was successful and a reduction in the ratio of 'quits' among the 'new hires' was observed.

Thus, the scene was set for the big push in 1977, involving 300 managers and supervisors and 3,500 hourly-paid employees. More than 250 workers expressed interest in becoming trainers, of whom 11 were selected for instructor training to go with the 11 chosen from the supervisors. The training lasted three days, for nine hours a day — with the ninth hour being paid at overtime rates. At an hourly rate of $7 per participant, the programme was a high investment.

The sessions covered three things: the concept of QWL; the plant and the functions of management and the union; and the problem-solving skills important in effective involvement. Specifically avoided was the solution of grievances or discussion of labour/management issues under dispute.

By the end of 1978, all the 3,500 employees had taken part. At that point, the plant was shut down for the introduction of an all-new model. In preparation, managers and hourly personnel evaluated hundreds of anticipated assembly operations. Together they discussed the best ways of setting up various operations on the line. What had been stimulated and prepared for by the training was now taking place in reality.

From being one of the worst plants in its quality performance, Tarrytown had become one of the best among the 18 plants in the division. Absenteeism fell to 2-3% and only 32 grievances were outstanding in December 1978. In May 1979, the new production line with a radically new car was working at projected line speed. Tarrytown had come trouble-free through a difficult transition that would have been disastrous under the old conditions.

The Tarrytown story shows what can be accomplished by the QWL approach. It also shows how long the process can take and how much effort must be put into overcoming entrenched attitudes. Labour/management antagonism runs deep and cannot be easily overcome.

The successes, however, are widespread and, from small beginnings in the 1970s, the trend towards employee involvement (EI) has grown rapidly. In an article in the *Harvard Business Review*, March/April 1985, 'From Control to Commitment in the Workplace', Richard Walton estimates that at least a thousand plants in the USA are in the process of making a comprehensive change towards EI.

In his *HBR* article, Walton contrasts the performance of two very similar plants in order to clarify the differences between management by control and management by commitment (see the Appendix to this chapter on pages 179-82). The one managed by commitment was superior on every measure of comparative performance from straight economics to absenteeism, turnover and safety. The commitment approach, as outlined, is strikingly similar to the model we have evolved here from best British practice.

The Japanese in the USA

As in Britain, it is the Japanese who have shown the way in applying the commitment model. One of the best examples is to be found in NUMMI (New United Motor Manufacturing Inc), a joint venture at Freemont in California between General Motors and Toyota. NUMMI employs 2,500 staff to produce 900 Chevrolet Novas per day, about twice the productivity of equivalent US plants. Indeed, GM employed 5,000 when it ran the plant alone before stopping production there early in 1982.

The UAW branch was one of the most militant. Absenteeism often exceeded 20% and hundreds of grievances were outstanding. Toyota was reluctant at first but finally agreed to recognize the UAW as the sole bargaining agent. The essential elements for creating commitment — employee involvement in decision-making, extensive training and the elimination of resented executive perks — were offered in return for more flexible working and abandonment of rigid rules.

There are, for instance, no parking places reserved for executives and no separate dining rooms. Managers all the way down from Tatusoro Toyoda, president of NUMMI and son of the founder, queue for their lunch in the canteen along with everyone else. At the same time, the beer bottles that used to litter the car park have disappeared — and the inside of the plant is spotless. Overall, absenteeism is down below 3% and there are usually no more than a dozen grievances pending

The number of job classifications was reduced from over 75 to 4 — one for production and three for skilled trades. Seniority rules were also eliminated. This prevents veteran employees from 'bumping' juniors with less seniority (i.e. having the right to a post, despite a lack of suitable experience) when they wish to make a job switch.

Such 'bumpings' have a cascade effect, causing disruption and retraining costs. Now workers with accumulated service can move into the job of their choice, but only when a vacancy occurs.

Great emphasis is placed on teamwork. The entire workforce is split into approximately 300 teams of five to eight people, each supervised by fellow hourly workers, with each member doing up to 15 jobs. They can stop the assembly line when components fail to meet design specifications. These teams take on much of management's shop-floor problem-solving responsibility.

Teams are responsible for checking quality and are continually finding ways to improve productivity. For instance, the 17 steps required to install a Nova door in 1985 have been reduced to 10 today. Such problem-solving skills require a relatively intelligent and well-trained workforce. Heavy emphasis is placed on finding intelligent, motivated workers and giving them plenty of training. It is not unusual for employees at Japanese companies to spend 20% of their first five years of employment in training!

Employee involvement at Ford

The power to stop the assembly line at NUMMI has also been given to workers at Ford's Edison plant in New Jersey. The 'stop button' at each work station is often used 10 to 20 times a day when a problem cannot be fixed in the 55 seconds allowed to each worker fitting bumpers and bonnets. Trouble shooters rush to help and usually within 20 seconds the line is running again.

Management was convinced that it would pay off handsomely if assemblers were treated like adults and allowed to stop the line to correct defects. The authority to control quality at source like this produced a fantastic response in the form of increased enthusiasm. Within four months, defects per car dropped from about 17 to less than one.

As this example shows, of the major traditional US industrial employers, Ford Motor Company has probably made the most dramatic progress towards employee involvement (EI). According to *Business Week*, thousands of teams of workers and supervisors at 86 of Ford's 91 plants and depots meet weekly to deal with production, quality and work-environment problems. As many as 34,000 hourly-paid employees — 30% of Ford's workforce — have some direct involvement in an EI project during the course of a year.

In spite of GM's earlier start with QWL in 1973, Ford's is a more pervasive and sustained effort. In late 1981, Ford made a corporate policy decision that a trained workforce is an asset to the company and that labour would no longer be treated as its most variable cost. That led to major job-security and training provisions in the 1982 contract.

Coming up to the present, Ford have recently scored a triumph with the cars in their Taurus/Sable line, which have had rave reviews and are the hottest sellers since Lee Iacocca's Mustang in the mid-1960s. This success was achieved by studying the customer, analyzing the competition and making quality the number one priority. Vital to this was streamlined operations and organization, prominently featuring EI in a 'Team Taurus' approach.

At the managerial level, Team Taurus took a 'programme management' approach. Representatives from all the various units — planning, design, engineering and manufacturing — worked together as a group. The team took final responsibility for the vehicle. Because all of the usually disjointed groups were intimately involved from the start, problems were resolved early on, before they caused a crisis.

Reverse engineering on competitors' products identified over 400 'best in class' features such as the Toyota Supra's fuel-gauge accuracy and the feel of the Audi 5000's accelerator pedal. Ford claim the Taurus/Sable meets or exceeds 80% of these 'best in class' features.

In keeping with its EI philosophy, assembly-line workers were asked for their advice even before the car was designed. Many suggestions were adopted. For example, the doors are now made from two panels instead of eight, and all bolts have the same size head to avoid grappling with different size spanners.

Ford are so pleased with this latest success of the 'management by teamwork' approach that they are adopting it across the board.

General Electric

The examples so far have been predominantly from the motor-car industry. The trend is much broader than that, however, as a brief look at General Electric will show.

Since Jack Welch took over as chairman of GE in 1982 there has been a transformation in the company's culture. Ambitious growth targets have been set, within the clear strategic objective of being number one or a close number two in any business engaged in. These businesses themselves have been separated into three major conceptual areas: core businesses, high technology and services.

Emphasis has been put on the importance of leadership, the sort of transforming leadership that gives people a feeling of 'ownership'. The key word 'ownership', in this context, has less to do with legal possession than with the freedom to take charge through the exercise of initiative and 'entrepreneurship'.

Great efforts have been made to push decision-making to the lowest appropriate level. The central planning staff has been cut from several hundred to less than one hundred. This is a radical move for a firm that 20 years ago was a pioneer in the establishment of strategic planning as a formal activity central to its management decision-making.

This shift has been part of the process of making GE 'light and agile' — a phrase Jack Welch much prefers to the more traditional and macho 'lean and mean'. 'Light and agile' reflects the importance of responsiveness and quick reaction to change. While efficiency is important, flexibility and creativity are even more so. 'Lean and mean' implies an attitude to people — be they employees, customers or even competitors — that is contrary to the values behind transforming leadership.

At the Louisville dishwasher plant in Kentucky, modernization has increased productivity by 25% and improved quality by a factor of ten, as judged by reductions in customer complaints. Machines are now constructed in 18 hours, as compared to a six-day crawl through the plant. This has reduced raw material stocks and inventory by more than half, from $9.5m to $3.9m.

Although investment and technology account for much of this improvement, it could not have been realized without a new approach to labour relations. The traditionally militant workforce was brought into discussions very early in the planning phase and participated enthusiastically.

Consequently, the changes were instituted with very few disputes. Strikes at the entire Louisville complex, producing other products too, have plummeted from 400,000 man/hours per year to less than 50,000.

The GE example points to a general phenomenon that is being increasingly recognized. The human side of automation, creating commitment in the workforce, is the key to making technology pay.

A changing approach to work organization

In the early 1980s, Shenandoah Life Insurance Co, installed a $2 million computer system in its processing and claims operation at its Roanoke headquarters in Virginia. Disappointingly, it still took 27 days, and handling by 32 clerks in three departments, to process a typical application for a policy conversion.

The problem lay in the bureaucratic maze of their segmented work organization. Even after automation, the processing clerks were, in effect, still passing bits of paper from person to person, but doing it electronically. The remedy required a radical reorganization of the work system.

The clerks were regrouped into semi-autonomous teams of five to seven members, with each team performing all the functions that were previously spread over three departments. In this way the computer was used to its full advantage, job satisfaction went up as people learnt new skills, and efficiency improved dramatically. Case-handling time dropped to two days and service complaints were practically eliminated. By 1986, Shenandoah was processing 50% more applications and queries with 10% fewer employees than in 1980.

Such integration of jobs makes it no longer possible to define jobs individually or measure individual performance. The abstract 'sociotechnical systems', as expounded by the Tavistock Institute forty years ago, are becoming clearly apparent with the advent of modern, computer-based automation. This requires a collection of people to manage a segment of technology and perform as a team.

Business Week commented on the changes which had slowly been taking place in industries like communications, cars and steel ever since the start of the movement for 'quality-of-working-life'. Even the unions had become more and more sympathetic to innovatory systems of working designed to create commitment. Jobs were broader-based and workers multiskilled, with increased scope for teamwork and management participation. Continuous on-the-job training, greater job security and payment schemes for group results had also transformed working life.

And yet such changes, *Business Week* continued, had been put in the shade by more recent developments inspired by the constant need for new products and worldwide competition. Problem-solving groups were a prominent example of such developments, which always aimed to enhance job satisfaction.

This approach is summed up in the table in the Appendix to this chapter on p183. Factories and offices following the new approach are proving to be 30% to 50% more productive than their conventional counterparts. Several hundred offices and factories, especially new, highly automated plants with small workforces of 25-500 people are using teamwork. In most cases, these teams manage themselves without first-line supervisors, determine their own work pace within parameters set by management, schedule their own vacations, and have a voice in hiring and firing team members and deciding when they are qualified enough to merit raises, within the bands laid down for their grade.

Many companies using teamwork tend to be reticent about revealing details because they believe it confers a significant competitive edge that they do not wish to lose. Proctor and Gamble, for example, have only recently confirmed that teamwork plants were 30% to 40% more productive than their traditional counterparts and significantly more able to adapt quickly to the changing needs of the business. Cummins Engine has three teamwork plants and is convinced that this is the most cost-effective way to operate. Tektronix Inc. converted a few years ago from assembly-line manufacturing in its metals group to teams. Each 'cell' of 6 to 12 workers turns out a product that can be manufactured in relatively few steps. One particular cell now turns out as many defect-free products in three days as an entire assembly line used to do in 14 days with twice as many people! In similar vein, Xerox Corp. began using teams in some of its operations a few years ago and has found them to be at least 30% more productive than conventionally organized operations.

As these examples show, there is a radical change in viewpoint taking place among American managers. The old adversarial approach, with workers being regarded as an easily replaceable pair of hands, is giving way to a commitment approach. In many cases, this is taken to the full extent of creating autonomous work groups and encouraging a wide degree of participation in all aspects of work and workplace design.

We in the UK ignore these developments in America at our peril. It has been too easy to dismiss moves in this direction by the Japanese as culturally specific and impossible to reproduce in the West. Realists that they are, and ever quick to adapt, the Americans have seen the falsity of this argument. Once convinced, they have not wasted any time in reacting. We must be equally quick and positive in our response if we are not to fall even further behind in the global competitiveness stakes.

Appendices

*The 'commitment' strategy**

Since the early 1970s, companies have experimented at the plant level with a radically different work-force strategy. The more visible pioneers — among them, General Foods at Topeka, Kansas; General Motors at Brookhaven, Mississippi; Cummins Engine at Jamestown, New York; and Proctor & Gamble at Lima, Ohio — have begun to show how great and productive the contribution of a truly committed work force can be.

Stimulated in part by the dramatic turnaround at GM's Tarrytown assembly plant in the mid-1970s, local managers and union officials are increasingly talking about common interests, working to develop mutual trust, and agreeing to sponsor quality-of-work-life (QWL) or employee involvement (EI) activities. Although most of these ventures have been initiated at the local level, major exceptions include the joint effort between the Communications Workers of America and AT & T to promote QWL throughout the Bell System and the UAW-Ford EI program.

More recently, a growing number of manufacturing companies has begun to remove levels of plant hierarchy, increase managers' spans of control, integrate quality and production activities at lower organizational levels, combine production and maintenance operations, and open up new career possibilities for workers. Some corporations have even begun to chart organizational renewal for the entire company. Cummins Engine, for example, has ambitiously committed itself to inform employees about the business, to encourage participation by everyone, and to create jobs that involve greater responsibility and more flexibility.

In this new commitment-based approach to the work force, jobs are designed to be broader than before, to combine planning and implementation, and to include efforts to upgrade operations, not

*Extracts, reproduced by permission, from 'From Control to Commitment in the Workplace' by Richard E. Walton. (*Harvard Business Review*, March/April 1985).

just maintain them. Individual responsibilities are expected to change as conditions change, and teams, not individuals, often are the organizational units accountable for performance. With management hierarchies relatively flat and differences in status minimized, control and lateral co-ordination depend on shared goals, and expertize rather than formal position determines influence.

Under the commitment strategy, performance expectations are high and serve not to define minimum standards but to provide 'stretch objectives', emphasize continuous improvement, and reflect the requirements of the marketplace. Accordingly, compensation policies reflect less the old formulas of job evaluation than the heightened importance of group achievement, the expanded scope of individual contribution, and the growing concern for such questions of 'equity' as gain sharing, stock ownership, and profit sharing.

Equally important to the commitment strategy is the challenge of giving employees some assurance of security, perhaps by offering them priority in training and retraining as old jobs are eliminated and new ones created. Guaranteeing employees access to due process and providing them the means to be heard on such issues as production methods, problem solving and human resource policies and practices is also a challenge. In unionized settings, the additional tasks include making relations less adversarial, broadening the agenda for joint problem solving and planning, and facilitating employee consultation.

Underlying all these policies is a management philosophy, often embodied in a published statement, that acknowledges the legitimate claims of a company's multiple stakeholders — owners, employees, customers, and the public. At the center of this philosophy is a belief that eliciting employee commitment will lead to enhanced performance. The evidence shows this belief to be well-grounded.

The 'control' strategy

The traditional — or control-oriented — approach to work-force management took shape during the early part of this century in response to the division of work into small, fixed jobs for which individuals could be held accountable. The actual definition of jobs, as of acceptable standards of performance, rested on 'lowest common denominator' assumptions about workers' skill and motivation. To monitor and control effort of this assumed caliber, management organized its own responsibilities into a hierarchy of specialized roles buttressed by a top–down allocation of authority and by status symbols attached to positions in the hierarchy.

For workers, compensation followed the rubric of 'a fair day's pay for a fair day's work' because precise evaluations were possible when individual job requirements were so carefully prescribed. Most managers had little doubt that labor was best thought of as a variable cost, although some exceptional companies guaranteed job security to head off unionization attempts.

In the traditional approach, there was generally little policy definition with regard to employee voice unless the work force was unionized, in which case damage control strategies predominated. With no union, management relied on an open–door policy, attitude surveys, and similar devices to learn about employees' concerns. If the work force was unionized, then management bargained terms of employment and established an appeal mechanism. These activities fell to labor relations specialists, who operated independently from line management and whose very existence assumed the inevitability and even the appropriateness of an adversarial relationship between workers and managers. . .

At the heart of this traditional model is the wish to establish order, exercise control, and achieve efficiency in the application of the workforce. Although it has distant antecedents in the bureaucracies of both church and military, the model's real father is Frederick W. Taylor, the turn–of–the–century 'father of scientific management', whose views about the proper organization of work have long influenced management practice as well as the reactive policies of the labor movement.

Recently, however, changing expectations among workers have prompted a growing disillusionment with the apparatus of control. At the same time, of course, an intensified challenge from abroad has made the competitive obsolescence of this strategy clear. A model that assumes low employee commitment and that is designed to produce reliable if not outstanding performance simply cannot match the standards of excellence set by world–class competitors. Especially in a high–wage country like the United States, market success depends on a superior level of performance, a level that, in turn, requires the deep commitment, not merely the obedience — if you could obtain it — of workers. And as painful experience shows, this commitment cannot flourish in a workplace dominated by the familiar model of control.

WHAT MANAGEMENT ASSUMES ABOUT WORKERS

OLD WAY Worker wants nothing from the job except pay, avoids responsibility, and must be controlled and coerced

NEW WAY Worker desires challenging job and will seek responsibility and autonomy if management permits

HOW THE JOB IS DESIGNED

OLD WAY Work is fragmented and deskilled. Worker is confined to narrow job. Doing and thinking are separated

NEW WAY Work is multiskilled and performed by teamwork where possible. Worker can upgrade whole system. Doing and thinking are combined

MANAGEMENT'S ORGANIZATION AND STYLE

OLD WAY Top-down military command with worker at bottom of many supervisory layers; worker is expected to obey orders and has no power

NEW WAY Relatively flat structure with few layers; worker makes suggestions and has power to implement changes

JOB TRAINING AND SECURITY

OLD WAY Worker is regarded as a replaceable part and is given little initial training or retraining for new jobs. Layoffs are routine when business declines

NEW WAY Worker is considered a valuable resource and is constantly retrained in new skills. Layoffs are avoided if possible in a downturn

HOW WAGES ARE DETERMINED

OLD WAY Pay is geared to the job, not the person, and is determined by evaluation and job classification systems

NEW WAY Pay is linked to skills acquired. Group incentive and profit-sharing plans are used to enhance commitment

LABOR RELATIONS

OLD WAY Labor and management interests are considered incompatible. Conflict arises on the shop floor and in bargaining

NEW WAY Mutual interests are emphasized. Management shares information about the business. Labor shares responsibility for making it succeed

DATA: RICHARD E. WALTON, HARVARD UNIVERSITY; BW

The changing approach to organizing work

13
Achieving a committed workforce

The simple, three-part model we have presented suggests that the companies we examined have built commitment on the foundation of three pillars: a sense of belonging — by *informing, involving,* and *giving a share in success;* a sense of excitement in the job — through *pride, trust* and *accountability for results* and confidence in management — through *authority, dedication* and *competence.*

As outlined in Chapter 12, the British experience in creating commitment is closely paralleled by US experience with QWL (quality of working life) and EI (employee involvement). The three pillars of the model fit equally well with this US experience. Collaborative agreements with the unions, consultation on plans and innovative reward systems have contributed to a sense of belonging and being valued, pillar I. Semi-autonomous team working, participatory problem-solving and work restructuring have contributed to a sense of excitement in the job, pillar II. As for pillar III, cross-cultural comparisons of confidence in management competence are difficult. There is no reason to suppose, however, that authority, dedication and competence are any less important in the USA than they are here.

The three-pillar model puts commitment into perspective. It shows how a wide variety of initiatives taken by management fit into a coherent picture, all pulling in the same direction and mutually reinforcing. Going beyond that, however, we have suggested in Chapter 1 how such new initiatives are taken in response to fundamental pressures in the business environment.

These pressures come from a variety of sources: most commonly, increasing technological complexity, the information/communications revolution, a rapidly-growing sector and global competition which demands both performance (productivity and quality) and innovation (creativity and openness to change).

Singly or in combination, these pressures build up to a realization of the strategic importance of commitment. No matter what strategic moves are made — retrenchment, new investment or shifts in product/market orientation — the benefits can only be fully achieved with the whole-hearted support of all those in the organization. The creation of commitment in the workforce comes to be seen as a vital component of any strategy in today's business environment.

The same pressures that lead to a realization of the strategic importance of commitment also very often lead to a major crisis that precipitates a change in top management or a complete organizational realignment. Indeed, the two often seem to go together: crisis forces a change of management, and the new management realizes that the strategic changes required can only be fully effective if they are complemented by a shift towards the creation of commitment.

All too often, however, this connection is not made. Management reacts to the crisis with measures to attack the symptoms. They do not analyze the forces that will inevitably blunt these measures if they are not implemented by a committed workforce. This failure to realize the strategic importance of commitment is probably even higher in firms that have not had a change of management as a result of the crisis that almost all firms have faced in recent years.

Be that as it may, commitment is now widely seen as being of fundamental strategic importance, particularly by the younger and better informed managers who have entered British boardrooms in countless recent shake-ups. Like everyone else, they can see what the Japanese are doing — and it has made them think. More important, they are aware of what is going on in the USA in response to this Japanese threat. And, apart from that, they understand the fundamental forces underlying the changes we have been facing.

All this represents a good start, but the creation of commitment is not something that can be done by a change of heart at the top alone. Top management can create the infrastructure, as it were, by instituting team briefing throughout an organization or setting up a productivity gain-sharing scheme for the entire workforce. But these initiatives imply an orientation towards people that requires a response in depth, from all levels of management, if it is to achieve its full impact.

This orientation can be summed up in the phrase 'faith in people'. There is no point in informing people or involving them unless one believes that they have something to offer and will respond. Giving a share in success only makes sense if one believes that the success is, in large part at least, due to people's increased input and application of talents. Without faith in people's ability one cannot give them pride or trust them and it is pointless trying to make them accountable for results.

It could be argued that having faith in people is the single underlying concept that generates all the actions, encompassed by the model, to make people feel they belong and become excited by their jobs. If that is so, it cannot stop at crisis-induced measures introduced by a new top management. Faith in people will have to become a way of life, embodied in the leadership behaviour of the entire management team, from top to bottom.

Getting commitment to be a way of life is an unending battle. It is always possible for otherwise progressive managements to temporarily slip up and violate their normally good practices. A vivid recent example is Jaguar cars. Their recovery is cited extensively in this book, and they have done a magnificent job of creating commitment in a typically disaffected British Leyland workforce. However, everyone is human and they precipitated a strike in October 1986 by sheer inattention.

Jaguar management in the summer of 1986 was riding high; productivity of current models had trebled since the troubled days of 1980, a new model had been launched to enthusiastic comments from the press and public, an independent survey showed employee attitudes to be excellent. The new model, named the XJ6 to commemorate its classic predecessor, had been launched in participatory style by pre-showings to huge assemblies of workers and their families. It had fantastic potential, with enormous productivity gains to be reaped from its advanced engineering design. An output of six cars per man per year was foreseen. Unthinkingly, industrial engineers, with all their time and motion paraphernalia, were launched on the production line to speed things up. Where was the participation in that? Where the involvement and trust? Forgotten in the euphoria — old habits run deep!

Winning commitment requires a radical change in point of view, apart from the innovative 'structural' changes that can be made, such as team briefing or productivity gain-sharing. Maintaining commitment requires that the changed point of view become instinctive, deep-rooted and permanent. A one-shot cosmetic boost will never fit the bill.

Tom Peters put his finger on the need for a deep-seated faith in people by identifying 'productivity through people' as one of the eight 'keys to excellence' in his 1982 bestseller *In Search of Excellence.* Since then, a host of books on leadership, by all the great names in behavioural science, has appeared. In their various ways they are all saying the same thing — leadership that builds on faith in people is able to achieve performance that goes beyond expectations.

Creating commitment requires a new approach to leadership throughout an organization to put this philosophy into practice. One such approach which we have developed is called *transforming leadership.* An outline of transforming leadership is presented here for the light it sheds on the difficult task of achieving a committed workforce.

Transforming leadership

Leadership implies a great deal more than management. Most of the world's great spiritual leaders would be quite unsuited to the management of an engineering company or a financial institution. On a more mundane level, political and military leaders have many management skills and are often able to make the transfer from one sphere to another. Nevertheless, success in one field does not guarantee success in the other.

Conversely, many people with management ability lack the leadership skills to rise to commanding positions in their company. There is more to being the chief executive of a major corporation than functional skill as a manager, no matter how well developed. The importance of those aspects of leadership that add an extra something to management are increasingly recognized. They are often referred to as 'transforming leadership', to distinguish them from the more traditional and managerial 'situational' leadership.

Traditional leadership models have focused on the choice of a leadership style to match, or be congruent with, the competence and commitment of the subordinates in performing a particular task. Because of this inward and specific focus on a particular situation, they are referred to as 'situational' models — looking at an individual or a group performing a given task in given circumstances. Situational leadership is managerial in that it is concerned with 'doing things right' and using the correct style to match the situation.

By contrast, transforming leadership is concerned with the leader's role in transcending current circumstances and creating a climate which changes perceptions of what is 'desirable, possible and necessary'. Transforming leadership is 'pathfinding', relating the individual to the organization, with a focus on values and 'doing the right thing'. Transforming leadership is concerned with the leader's *role* in forming and guiding the organization's culture; in contrast, situational, or congruent, leadership is concerned with the leader's *style* in specific circumstances.

Just as the congruent leadership style can vary from autocratic to participatory, the transforming leadership role can be exercised in a participatory and integrative way or an autocratic and interventionist way. These two ways of performing the transforming leadership role are given descriptive names in our model of transforming leadership.

The first we call a 'visionary/enabler' who has faith in people while simultaneously creating a vision to inspire them and enabling them to contribute their full talents to achieving it. By contrast, we call the other a 'controller/manipulator' who seeks transformation by imposing his or her solutions through control and manipulation.

Both types of transforming leader are pathfinders, to use Leavitt's term in his book of that title, concerned with seeking the way and pointing their organizations in new directions. The contrast lies in how they do it.

The controller/manipulator's way is illustrated below. Leadership is concentrated at the top with the controller/manipulator driving the organization. It is a very egocentric and hierarchical approach, with the subordinates reflecting the leader.

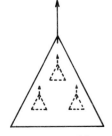

CONTROLLER/MANIPULATOR

- DRIVES ORGANIZATION
- EGOCENTRIC
- HIERARCHICAL
- SUBORDINATES REFLECT LEADER
- CONCENTRATED AT TOP
- TDC

By contrast, the second diagram portrays the visionary/enabler's way of providing transforming leadership. Leadership is seen as being diffused throughout the organization, with the visionary/

enabler channelling it together. It is a very participatory approach, with the leader facilitating and embodying the subordinates.

VISIONARY/ENABLER
- CHANNELS ABILITIES
- FACILITATES
- PARTICIPATORY
- LEADER EMBODIES SUBORDINATES
- DIFFUSED THROUGHOUT
- TLC

The visionary/enabler has faith in people which is exhibited by showing them 'tender loving care' — TLC, to use the common abbreviation. This is contrasted with the TDC of the controller/manipulator. These initials were coined by Tom Peters in *Passion for Excellence*, the sequel to *In Search of Excellence*. They stand for 'thinly disguised contempt' — the attitude that the controller/manipulator takes towards people.

These two extremes of controller/manipulator and visionary/enabler should be thought of as stereotypes fixing the opposite ends of the range in transforming roles. Douglas McGregor had a similar intention of fixing extremes when, in his Theory X and Theory Y, he mapped out the contrasting views that managers may take of people's attitude to work. Just as no one takes a purely Theory X or Theory Y view of people, no leader is purely controller/manipulator or visionary/enabler.

We feel that to create a committed workforce and derive the full benefit, the transforming leadership of the visionary/enabler is essential throughtout the management hierarchy. Without it, the commitment model can only be put into effect by directions from top management. These will never have their full impact if they are not supported by leadership at all levels that puts faith in people.

Let us now take a moment to look at the two contrasting roles in more detail.

The controller/manipulator

Thinly disguised contempt is an attitude fairly widespread among British managers. They do not actually feel that workers have got much to contribute. The idea of informing them and involving them so that they have a chance to contribute to decision-making and the achievement of objectives would seem futile: nothing would come of it — except trouble! Time would be wasted in fruitless talk, giving people a chance — which they would surely exploit — to dodge work and malinger. If, by some wild chance, something constructive did come of it, this would merely be taken as an excuse to demand a raise or some concession on work practices.

Successful participation would also be highly threatening, in that the leader would no longer be the all-wise boss on whose wisdom all success depends. This has frequently been reported as a problem for middle managers in organizations where the lower echelons have been encouraged to contribute through such devices as autonomous work groups, suggestion schemes and quality circles.

The 'know-all' — one kind of controller/manipulator — is prone to this. Proud of his technical or functional expertise, the know-all insists that every decision or recommendation should conform to his view. Although he may give lipservice to the idea of subordinates joining in decision-making, everyone knows that nothing will come of it.

The know-all may sincerely ask for suggestions and new ideas, but somehow few are forthcoming. His subordinates have found out the hard way that no matter how much effort they put into the hard slog of producing ideas, the time will never be ripe to adopt them. No matter how brilliant the idea, if it does not conform exactly to the know-all's view of the world, countless excuses for delay will be found.

In this way, people become discouraged and stop responding to appeals for ideas and suggestions. This lack of response, in turn, reinforces the know-all's view that subordinates have nothing to contribute and leads to the martyr's cry: 'Why do I have to do everything around here? Nobody ever has a single worthwhile idea! Everything is left to me . . . if it wasn't for my expertise . . . etc.'

As good people get frustrated and demotivated, success becomes limited by the abilities and understanding of the know-all. If times are stable and he is, in fact, all-wise, this may be satisfactory. Unfortunately, this is rarely, if ever, the case. Even if it were, there is still a tendency to get locked into old and familiar solutions based on the know-all's unaugmented expertise.

Young managers, newly promoted because of some technical or functional skill, are prone to be know-alls. Proud of their skill, they guard it jealously and are reluctant to admit that they may need help, for fear of being thought inadequate or unable to cope. After a time, however, they mature and take a more relaxed view. In these fast-changing times, too, it is not long before their expertise has decayed and they are no longer the whizz-kid with all the answers. It is then time to beware of the related danger of continuing to be a controller/manipulator by becoming a ringmaster.

The ringmaster admits that others have technical or functional expertise that he lacks, but he compensates for this by extreme activity in reshaping relationships. In his eyes, the success of the group is entirely due to the energy and skill with which he, the ringmaster, motivates people, resolves interpersonal problems and arbitrates disputes.

No responsibility is put on the group to regulate their own behaviour. Consequently, they never learn to solve their own problems. On the contrary, they are free to indulge in all sorts of political games-playing and jockeying for position. Since the ringmaster has taken responsibility for arbitrating disputes, they can all be as stubborn as they like — the ringmaster can always be relied upon to render a judgement to break the deadlock.

Since there is no incentive to take a wider perspective, the ringmaster's subordinates often revert to seeking ways to beat the system while doing the minimum to get by. The ringmaster then has to redouble his efforts in order to maintain performance. This is the classic recipe for a self-fulfilling prophecy. All the burdens of maintaining the group and solving its internal disputes rest on the ringmaster. He becomes overloaded and is convinced that his subordinates are incapable of showing initiative or taking responsibility.

The know-all and the ringmaster are versions of the controller/manipulator. The controller side puts emphasis on setting limits and making rules, giving much attention to preventing deviations from those rules and limits. A feeling of control is enhanced by accepting only his or her own view, being slow to change and wary of ideas. All this breeds alienation and a 'them and us' spirit in the subordinates.

Similarly, the manipulator side is paternalistic, playing employees off against each other. Responsibility is withheld, with an emphasis on exploiting current abilities rather that developing talents. In this 'keep 'em guessing' way, a group of minions is created which is kept off balance in a climate of fear and uncertainty.

The visionary/enabler

The visionary/enabler is concerned with values, those of the individual and those of the organization. One major concern is to bring those two together — helping the individual to relate his or her values to those of the organization. People, even in these days of high unemployment, are less and less inclined to accept work that conflicts with their basic values. The visionary/enabler articulates a vision that reflects the values of the organization and expresses them in a way that is compatible with those of the subordinates.

A clear vision, set down in a mission statement, helps to channel people's energies constructively. Having something clear and compelling to strive for takes people out of themselves and releases their energy in pursuit of the ideal. This is particularly so if the mission statement is backed up by well-defined and quantified goals — goals that stretch people while still being feasible.

The visionary/enabler subtly creates a climate of success. The feeling of goals accomplished is a powerful factor in the release of energy. Everyone is made to feel that their marginal contribution is important to the continuing high performance. Awards are created so that contributions can be acknowledged and behaviour reinforced. Stories of exemplary 'heroes' are composed and kept in circulation.

The psychological attitude of a group is crucial to its success. Mike Brearley, who lost only four of the eighteen Tests he captained, tells the story of the England side in Australia who called the seat near the dressing-room door, for the next batsman in, the 'condemned cell'. To no one's surprise, the batsmen performed accordingly! Similarly, a Northants team, with only 76 runs to score in 40 overs, was reported to be asking itself 'Who's going to score these runs for us?' Hardly surprisingly, they were all out for 41 in 36 overs!

The visionary/enabler champions ideas. Ideas are fragile flowers, easily crushed by ridicule or neglect. It is well-established that most successful innovations are supported by a volunteer champion who protects them from attack, ensures they have access to resources and encourages them through difficulties.

As an enabler, the visionary/enabler treats people as individuals and develops their talents. He creates a team that is able to exercise self-regulation of its own interpersonal relationships — with the vision, expressed in the mission statement, as a guide. The visionary/

enabler is willing to give early responsibility, taking advantage of the Pygmalion effect. It is found that people will generally try to live up to high expectations. In striving to meet them, they will frequently produce results that astound themselves and others.

All this is done in the context of clearly defined goals. The creation off a vision, to give the group an overall purpose, is no substitute for quantified goals that give expression to short-term targets compatible with that vision. Without this attention to specific goals, the vision can become an abstraction that gives comfort but does not provide specific impetus to action.

The visionary/enabler is a combination of the 'contributor' and 'catalyst'. If the leader has some technical or functional expertise, and it is most unusual if he does not, it is made available to the group as a contribution to the problems to be solved. The contributor is open to the ideas of others: if new information or a better solution is put forward, he is happy to accept it.

Similarly, the catalyst makes himself available to help in the solution of interpersonal problems and the resolution of disputes or conflicts. He does not, however, impose solutions and avoids being drawn into arbitration. Rather, he pushes responsibility on to the group so that they develop their own interpersonal skills, using the vision as a guide to their choices.

To sum up, the controller/manipulator behaves as a know-all or ringmaster. Ideas that do not fit in are rejected, and control is established to ensure conformity. Groups and individuals are manipulated, paternalistically and with thinly disguised contempt, to maintain control. By contrast, the visionary/enabler behaves as a contributor and catalyst. He creates a vision for his subordinates that draws them into the organization, making them feel that they belong and have some excitement in their jobs. At the same time, he treats people as individuals, developing their talents, enabling them to contribute to the full.

Although the controller/manipulator can be a transforming leader in that he or she looks outwards and is pathfinding, the way this is done is at odds with the needs of our changing business environment. Whether there are circumstances in which the controller/manipulator is the optimum transforming role is beyond the scope of this chapter. Suffice it to say that the controller/manipulator's is, clearly, not the best approach to the creation of a committed workforce. That role is best performed by the visionary/enabler.

Transforming leadership as a concept is rapidly gaining ground in management practice throughout the world. The formulation presented here, focussing on the visionary/enabler, is particularly supportive of the commitment model we have described. Training young managers to behave as visionary/enablers helps them to create a sense of belonging and excitement in the job. Informing people and involving them is at the heart of visionary/enabling, as is trusting them, stimulating pride and making them accountable for results.

If commitment is to be created and its full impact enjoyed, a conscious effort is needed, through a co-ordinated training campaign, to reorient the entire management team to the transforming role of the visionary/enabler. This will ensure that faith in people becomes the guiding principle which will inspire leadership at every management level.

Training

Apart from a re-orientation programme for the management team to implant transforming leadership, training is a key component in the creation of commitment.

Many managers, particularly the controller/manipulators, claim that creating commitment by putting faith in people is a futile activity. Armed with a heavy dose of thinly disguised contempt, they assert that most workers are too ignorant, lazy or uneducated to respond in any worthwhile or significant way. This is largely a self-fulfilling prophecy.

Because no potential has been seen in the workforce, there has been very little effort put into training. Consequently, the workforce does have less to contribute than if it were properly trained. That limited ability to contribute is then used as a justification for not training — and another twist is added to the negative spiral.

A more reasonable reaction would be to put faith in people, tapping whatever potential they presently have, while providing the training necessary to raise their ability to contribute. This is not an idealistic or altruistic attitude. Vastly increased training is required, anyway, if we are to meet the challenge posed by the forces, previously identified, in the business environment.

Bryan Nicholson, chairman of the Manpower Services Commission, found himself in hot water, recently, when he was reported to have said that Britain's workforce, from top management down, was a bunch of 'thickies'.

What he actually said was: 'When you compare Britain's adult workforce, from top management down, with those in our main competitor countries, we emerge as a bunch of thickies. I am not talking about intelligence or natural ability, I am talking about skills and qualifications, I am talking, in a word, about training'.

We are going to have to do better. A study of 45 matched firms in Britain and Germany, producing comparable products with similar equipment, showed German productivity to be 63% higher. The difference could only be put down to better education and training.

Workers at GM's new front-axle plant at Saginaw in Michigan are being trained for a full year before the plant opens. In our Pilkington case history, a tremendous effort was put into training so that one grade of technician was able to do all the jobs previously covered by eight grades.

The same goes for management. Employees throughout their career at IBM get as much as 40 days of off-the-job training a year. There are firms in Britain where the managers have had no training at all. It is all part of the glorious British cult of the amateur, summed up in the typical viewpoint that 'We are practical chaps and learn how to manage by actually doing it, we do not need any of your fancy concepts and long-haired jargon.' This optimism has proved strikingly successful, as our machine-tool, motor-car, motor-cycle, shipbuilding and textile industries demonstrate! The dreadful lack of basic management competence is neatly illustrated by two stories publically told in the management columns of national newspapers in the last year or so.

One of Britain's leading companies was delighted with a senior management programme put on for them in the early 1980s by London Business School. The so-called 'marketing concept' came to them as a revelation and stimulus to great new things — they were sure it would make a tremendous difference to their future strategy. The only trouble is that this idea has been commonplace in progressive companies throughout the world since the middle 1960s.

The managing director of a major UK electronics firm was publicly quoted in 1986 as saying that 'I shudder every time I hear the word training'. He did, however, have the grace to recant, after a high-level management development programme, in the face of evident gaps in the firm's management skills. It was admitted that 'Market share was ignored' and 'that the ability to practise market segmentation, product positioning and other basic-marketing techniques was woefully inadequate'.

There is a long way to go in many firms before management competence is such that it warrants the confidence of the workforce — Pillar III in the model. Until management thoroughly understands what marketing is all about, has absorbed the latest manufacturing techniques and started thinking strategically about its competitive position, it has no right to be contemptuous of the abilities of its workforce.

This is particularly true in view of the pitiful amount that it puts into training, compared to what is required and what our competitors provide. Where will the money come from for all this training? That is, basically, a short-term cash-flow problem. Ultimately, the training will pay for itself — many times over. Sit down and calculate what a 5% or 10% improvement in productivity would be worth to your operation. Then reflect on the fact that 73% of workers felt they could do substantially more in their jobs, and 17% twice as much. A 5-10% increase in productivity should only scratch the surface of the total potential improvement. In that light, the cost of training within a commitment programme comes into perspective.

Think, too, of the direct and indirect benefits of higher quality, reduced labour turnover, lower absenteeism, and less waste — both of material and effort. What would flexibility in manning, better work practices and co-operation in making changes mean to you? Innovative suggestions from the workforce have saved companies hundreds of thousands of pounds — how many ideas are latent in *your* organization waiting for the right climate to emerge?

The potential is huge. The evidence is overwhelming. All that is needed is the courage and imagination to do it.

Commitment and the Personnel Manager

Since this book is appearing under the imprint of the Institute of Personnel Management, it is appropriate to think for a moment of the specific role of the personnel manager in creating commitment. Although this is, fundamentally, a line management task, there is much that the personnel manager can do to give support.

To start with, consider the first pillar of commitment — the vital sense of belonging. The feeling of belonging to an elite group can be immensely enhanced by maintaining high entry standards and insisting on conformity to group norms and standards. Careful selection and proper 'socialization' are essential elements.

Care in selection is doubly important in view of the trend towards fewer core employees, but of higher quality and flexibility. In view of this, it is, perhaps, surprising how little attention is paid to recruitment and selection. Few firms adopt multiple screening methods or make extensive use of psychometric tests and assessment centres.

The creation of commitment can be greatly assisted by rigorous attention to the selection of new recruits for an organization. They would be subject to formal tests, conscientious reference checks and extensive interviews. The interviewers would come from a pool of managers, seconded to the responsibility for a period of a year or two, who would have received adequate training in interview techniques. They would have a common view, based on first-hand experience, of the committed environment into which the recruit was coming and would be equipped, by training, to assess how well the candidates' personalities and experiences fitted them to join.

Ample opportunity, in the course of in-depth interviews, would be given for candidates to 'de-select' themselves. Although annoying, it is better to lose unsuitable candidates before they join than go to the expense of training and integrating them only to have them leave, or be fired, prematurely. Broken engagements are preferable to messy divorces.

Similarly, the process of socialization is one to which personnel managers can make a vital contribution. Careful screening will have sent the message: 'You have got to be special to join.' This is reinforced by a properly implemented induction programme in the first few months — designed to emphasize the newcomer's ignorance of the organization's norms and values and the need to absorb them. This process is complemented by extensive, practical training in a core discipline of the business. Promotion is then closely tied to the subsequent track record of success, based on carefully designed systems to measure operational results.

The aim of socialization is to establish a base of attitudes, habits and values that foster co-operation, integrity and communication. Contrary to some expectations, this does not stifle innovativeness. The companies with strong socialization traditions are long-lasting and successful firms like 3M, IBM and Philips. They are highly innovative and remain so by fostering social rules that reward innovation.

Looking now at the second pillar of commitment — a sense of excitement in the job — personnel management can contribute to commitment by helping to cultivate 'obsessions' that focus on values and give meaning to everything that is done. Common examples are quality, customer service and technological excellence. An obsession with such values supports line managers who are attempting to practise transforming leadership by behaving as visionary/enablers.

The personnel department is well placed to take a broad view of the firm and help line management in the articulation of its mission statement. Very often, functional bias will distort the view of line management. The marketing department may favour quality, while the salespeople emphasize customer service, and production focusses on technological superiority. Such viewpoints may well provide mission statements for parts of the organization, but they must be integrated to provide a proper strategic balance.

Personnel can also help in the diffusion and assimilation of mission statements by building them into the entire selection, induction and training sequence. Key elements of the firm's overall mission can, with a little imagination, be made the subject of specially tailored courses and seminars. This reinforces the continuous message that is incorporated in the normal training flow.

The appraisal system should be re-examined to ensure that due weight is given to activities and practices which reinforce participation and teamwork. As at Jaguar, for instance, managers should be encouraged to push responsibility for quality down the line: 'Get it right first time!' Involving people entails risks for busy managers and will be avoided unless it is encouraged. Encouragement can be given by specific recognition of such behaviour at appraisal. If this is reflected, as appropriate, in reward and promotion, it will in time demonstrate and reinforce the firm's priorities.

The third pillar of commitment — confidence in management's leadership — requires that personnel management takes a broad firm-wide view to offset some of the inherent weaknesses of line management.

In many organizations, the way to the top is seen to be through mobility and the gathering of experience. This results, especially for rapidly growing firms, in managers moving frequently. The average tenure of a management position can be as short as eighteen months to two years. Such rapid movement frequently produces a very short-term outlook. Decisions are based on their immediate impact rather than the long-term benefit to the organization. The personnel department can contribute to the creation of commitment by taking steps to offset this short-term bias of rapidly moving managers.

For example, the benefits of training often appear long after the event. Neglect of training and development should not be used to give an apparent boost to current operating performance. Personnel, by keeping proper records and monitoring the progress of individuals, can ensure that managers do not reap short-term savings at the expense of long-term benefit.

On a more general level, personnel should seek ways to offset the authoritarian bias that often creeps into the leadership style of quickly moving managers. Relationships take time to build and the pay-off from an atmosphere of trust and co-operation is not immediate. In the short term, the leader can often achieve results without expending effort to elicit a whole-hearted contribution from his team. There is, thus, a temptation for rapidly moving managers to fall into an authoritarian leadership style to the neglect of long-term relationships and efficiency.

To sum up, every effort should be made to ensure that the management reward and appraisal system transcends narrow, quantifiable short-term results. More weight should be given to longer-term efforts to create commitment and the basis for excellence through innovation, adaptability and efficiency.

One final note of caution: in spite of the recent talk of excellence and the examples of Japanese success, Western line management has a long and inglorious 'macho' tradition. The image of the effective manager is of a 'shaker and mover' rather than a consensus builder, a 'results-oriented achiever' rather than a developer and encourager.

From this perspective, the personnel department is often viewed with suspicion bordering on contempt. Such views, however unpalatable, must be confronted by realistic personnel managers. In focusing on the importance of commitment, a double challenge is faced — to overcome the macho self-image of some line managers while not reinforcing their view of the personnel function as wet and irrelevant. One of the best guarantees of succeeding in this is to ensure that the personnel manager has a firm grasp of the links between the organization's strategic objectives and the contribution that can come, in improved performance and greater innovation, from a committed workforce. Being concerned with people and gaining their commitment is not a 'soft option', it is a vital component of success in our competitive world. By helping to articulate the firm's strategy and making it a guide to action in the development of people, the charge of impractical 'do-good-ism' can be avoided.

14
Observations on the evolution of British management

The company case studies cited in this book have provided support for the model of commitment that we have presented. Indeed, the model itself was originally devised to help pull together the diverse experience of these companies, as presented to a series of conferences.

In visiting the companies to gather more details and update the stories, a great deal of background material was revealed that it has not been possible to include here. The final versions of the company cases, as approved by the companies, do not contain a record of the many informal discussions that helped to put the case histories into perspective.

In casual chats and off-the-cuff remarks, revealing glimpses were often given of the forces underlying some of the more dramatic turn-arounds. A frank aside, interjected into a conversation, would illuminate the relationships and motivations behind a complex series of negotiations. Confidential briefings provided a rich supplement to help put a complex and evolving story into context.

The privilege of having a detailed and high-level insight into the management thinking of a significant cross-section of British companies does not often occur. It seemed to us a pity not to reflect on this exposure to see if it contained any patterns, trends or themes. The opportunity, too good to be missed, has tempted us to write this final chapter.

It is only fair to point out that speculation will be rife. Our own prejudices and stereotypes will have conditioned what we heard, what we retained as significant and how we have woven it into a pattern. Our justification is that the speculation is based on first-hand observation, involving many man-weeks of interaction with over a hundred managers from a score of British companies, of all sizes and many industries — both service and manufacturing.

Manufacturing industry

Considering the traumas of the past decade, is it reasonable to suppose that manufacturing management now believes firmly in commitment? Can it be true that the very managers who pruned the workforce so ruthlessly and so firmly reasserted their managerial authority are now dedicated to creating commitment? How can one expect a workforce, battered by waves of redundancies, to respond to a management that has taken such drastic corrective action, often arbitrarily and with very little apparent consideration? These are some of the questions that emerge when reflecting on the implications of the material gathered for this book. The paradox seems to be real.

In the seventies there were massive redundancies in industry and commerce. Management acted in a manner which could only be described as ruthless. Yet, today, the level of performance and commitment in many of those firms is higher than it has ever been — as high as in those firms which avoided the worst of the traumas. Are we to suppose that one way to generate commitment is through a programme of massive redundancies? Can pride and employee commitment be generated through fear?

There are those who would see a great deal of merit in the idea that a short sharp shock, followed by a good dose of discipline, is all that is required to knock some sense into a recalcitrant workforce. Although we do not share this viewpoint, there is no doubt that there has been a profound change in the industrial-relations climate in the last ten years. Militancy has declined and the strike record is better now than it has been since before the Second World War.

This change in climate, due fundamentally to a shift in our national economic circumstances, can be traced through a number of key events. The coal strike of the early 70s and the three-day week set the scene for the 'winter of discontent' a few years later. This era amply demonstrated how bad things could be. Then, in 1980, the steel strike was lost and a new sense of realism in that industry presaged a turn of the tide.

At the same time, British Leyland was being brought 'back from the brink', to quote the title of Michael Edwardes's book. One key event there was the sacking of 'Red Robbo' for opposing the restructuring plan that had been accepted by a ballot of the workforce. To challenge militant shop stewards in this way had, until then, been unthinkable.

Finally, there was the miners' strike. By the narrowest of margins, the almost mythical power of a traditionally militant group to hold the country to ransom was curbed. Significant in this victory was the lack of support from the power workers and the willingness of lorry drivers to take risks in delivering coal. Even more remarkable was the solidarity of the steelworkers in protecting their newly won job security. They did not want the sacrifices they had made to produce a viable industry thrown away to satisfy the political aims of Arthur Scargill.

No doubt some have taken advantage of this change in climate. Charges that 'macho' managers are squeezing unreasonable concessions from an intimidated workforce are frequently heard. Any doing so, however, are not typical of the managers in the companies providing our case examples. These managers certainly acted with determination but, in our view, their motivation was much more complex than a mere 'macho' reversion to type.

How manufacturing management rendered itself helpless

A first step in resolving the paradox is to consider why management acted so ruthlessly and with so little consultation in reducing numbers in the late seventies and early eighties. Basically, we feel that this was the desperate response to crisis of managers who had allowed themselves to be rendered helpless by cumulative weakness over a long period.

There is no need to dwell on the crisis. The two oil-price shocks, uncontrolled inflation, world-wide recession and intensifying competition from all sides combined to deliver a death blow to many in British industry. Cosmetic responses would no longer suffice. Drastic action was required. But management was in no position to act in anything but an arbitrary way. To understand why, one has only to reflect on what has happened to British industry since the Second World War.

The post-war recovery and rapid growth in world trade created a period of prosperity in which the seeds of much future trouble were sown. It was easier to yield concessions on wage-rates, manning levels and working practices than to face conflict to preserve a principle. Management all too often took the easy way out.

Low productivity may have meant higher costs, but these could be passed on to the consumer in higher prices. Poor practices might have contributed to low reliability, but the market was buoyant enough to cushion any negative effect on sales. Resistance to change may have been hampering modernization, but Far-Eastern competition, although increasing, was not yet global in scope — the reckoning could be postponed. All the costs of inefficiency could be borne by the consumer. If this burden became too high, the taxpayer could be called upon — directly for the nationalized industries or via various subsidies and grants for the private sector.

The unions steadily increased their power and influence, not hesitating to resort to strikes where necessary to reinforce the message. Employment legislation grew more complex, giving rise to industrial-relations (IR) departments. Management allowed itself to be rendered progressively more helpless. Contact with the workforce was channelled through the unions and shop stewards. Contact with the unions often became the exclusive preserve of the IR department.

Thus, management became doubly isolated from direct contact with the workforce. The unions monopolized face-to-face communication with their members, while negotiations with the union were increasingly in the hands of the IR department. Michael Edwardes vividly described in his book, *Back from the Brink*, how permission had to be obtained from the British Leyland shop stewards before he could go on to the shop floor at Longbridge.

The climate was increasingly one of confrontation. The gulf between management and the workforce widened. The employees, or rather the union shop stewards, ran the factories. Management had lost the ability to communicate with its own employees: it had to speak through shop stewards, via the IR department. Demarcation and restrictive practices were rife. People at work, including managers, were seriously underemployed. Productivity was low.

Management's helplessness was compounded by the low level of aspiration that was the norm in the UK. If the workforce had better understood where its own best interests lay — or if management had succeeded better in creating this understanding — it could have exploited the post-war boom to expand markets through high levels of efficiency and hence ensured high earnings. It seemed, however, not to be interested in doing so. When workers could control earnings — for example, through piecework — they very often chose to establish norms significantly below those that were possible (to smooth out wages and avoid peaks and troughs).

In taking this line, it could be said that the workforce was acting in good faith, since they believed that they were protecting employment. They were guided by their trade-union leaders, who believed in the 'lump of labour' fallacy, the idea that there are only so many jobs to go round. This means that the national cake can only be shared — it is not really capable of expansion by creativity, innovation or flexible responses to market needs.

Of course, such attitudes, as can now so clearly be seen, did not protect employment — they destroyed it. The onslaught of increasing international competition and the oil-price shocks caught much of British industry unprepared. The writing had been on the wall from at least the early sixties, but it had been ignored. Suddenly there was no escape. This was the point at which management acted with a ruthless decisiveness that must have surprised even themselves.

Authoritarianism, although inadequate, may perhaps have been the only practical response available at that time of crisis in the seventies: industrial relations were so bad there was no other way forward. There was frequently no trust between manager and managed. Often there was very little communication. What really was required was a sea-change in attitudes on both sides — and fast. However, the practical reality was that, for many firms, up to half the distrustful workforce was going to be forced out of a job in very short order. In the circumstances there was really nothing else to do but act quickly and with determination — i.e. be authoritarian.

Does this authoritarian response to crisis reveal management's true disposition? Some would say that it does. In our view, however, it was the desperate response of a management that had allowed itself to become progressively more helpless. Faced by crisis, management finally galvanized itself into action. However, the necessary conditions of trust and communication needed for consultation did not exist. Managers had no choice, therefore, but to act arbitrarily.

One could, with some justice, argue that it was their own fault that they found themselves in this unfortunate position. But this does not mean that they proved themselves to be fundamentally authoritarian. They were trapped into behaving that way when their self-induced helplessness was confronted by a do-or-die crisis.

The beginning of a new approach

In our view, the crisis — and the way they were forced to respond to it — made management realize how helpless they had become. They realized that their expedient granting of concessions and lack of insistence on competitive standards had deepened the crisis. They realized that they had lost touch with the workforce and that confrontation and resistance prevailed, rather than trust and co-operation. They recognized that these problems could only be corrected by an entirely new approach.

This realization was reinforced by what they had seen of the way the Japanese were able to achieve unheard-of levels of productivity and quality. It was further reinforced by trends in the environment towards greater technological complexity, the information/ communications revolution and shorter product life cycles, as outlined in Chapter 1.

But it is equally true to say that most of the workforce recognized the new realities. This can be seen in the facts that they have become so much more flexible and that productivity has risen two to three times. It can be seen as well in the extremely positive response there has been to available training opportunities.

At Hardy Spicer, eight hundred employees applied for forty re-training places. At Rothmans, one hundred and twenty employees out of less than a thousand applied for pre-management training. At Jaguar, over 20% of the workforce are involved in the firm's 'open learning' programme.

In fact, the old days of restrictive practices were extremely frustrating for many employees. As the survey results quoted in Chapter 1 show, they did not enjoy working below their true potential. They were prevented from giving of their best by 'custom and practice'. In the words of an employee made redundant from the Llanwern steelworks: 'We knew that things could not go on as they had been. Our wives used to tell us that we never did a full day's work for our money and they were right. It had to change. People had to go or there would have been nothing left — nothing for anybody. I was sorry to go, but it was the right thing.'

Thus, the crisis precipitated new perceptions on both sides that brought them much closer together. Management and the workforce came to realize much more clearly that they are all in the same boat. It is not too fanciful to liken this boat to a 'survival ark' afloat on a sea of competition. Everyone has their part to play and it requires the best from everyone if the ark is to stay afloat. Graham Day, chief executive of Austin Rover, described the situation recently: 'Everyone's job is now on the line, including my own.'

Thinking in terms of the survival ark focusses attention on beating the competition by serving the customer. There is no place for restrictive practices, demarcation disputes or reluctance to change — and these are disappearing. At the same time, management must realize that everyone has something to contribute. They must create the conditions and climate in which this contribution can be made. The talents and energies of the entire workforce must be channelled towards maximum efficiency and creativity.

So although management reacted to the crisis with the necessary ruthlessness, this does not automatically mean that they were seeking authoritarian control. The terms on which jobs were offered to the survivors of the seventies were not that they should obey every management instruction without question but that people should be flexible, learn new skills, train their colleagues and contribute to the formulation of management decisions.

Understanding this last point is crucial to understanding the evolving relationship between managers and employees in many organizations. The point is not that employees make decisions? It is that good managers actively seek out employee opinions so that the decisions they — the managers — make are better informed. This is a basis on which employees can easily contribute. They know that although they will not be responsible for the decisions, they can contribute to their formulation.

Problems arise when employees do not understand this way of contributing to the decision-making process. Relations between management and employees are soured when the employee feels able to say: 'They consulted me, but they had made up their own mind already anyway.' The corollary is that managers must be prepared to change their mind if others' ideas are better than their own. They must also be prepared to give credit to others when their ideas are adopted. The transforming leadership approach, as outlined in Chapter 13, provides guidance for both managers and subordinates in making this new relationship productive.

Much of the cynicism about participation arises because of misconceptions about the strengths and limitations of involvement. It is felt by those who misunderstand it to be either a management trick to give employees the illusion that their opinions matter or an abdication by management of the authority which they as managers should exercise.

As in all things, a balance has to be struck. Managers have to reach a deeper understanding of what the workforce can contribute and workers have to appreciate the limits of their influence.

Generally speaking, the closer one reaches the physical workplace, the higher will be the direct experience of those working there. Consequently, they will have more to contribute, and greater weight should be given to their contribution. As many of the examples in this book show, managers are becoming more and more aware of just how much shopfloor workers can contribute. It is a commonplace for managers to be astounded by the depth and value of the suggestions that are made — once the employees become convinced that their opinions are valued and will be listened to.

On the other hand, employees must be aware that not all suggestions are economically viable or will fit into the overall strategic picture. The more sweeping and far-reaching the suggestion, the more likely it is to have unanticipated ramifications. There is a natural human tendency to see everything from one's own local perspective. This gives rise to a corresponding tendency to question decisions based on a broader view that one is not aware of or does not understand. This narrowness of view and lack of understanding can be minimized by making sure that the workforce is fully informed of the broader context within which decisions are made. It also helps, of course, if the overall strategy of the business is sound and exhibits the hallmarks of professional management.

More professional management

There can be no doubt that, in all but the smallest firms, the general level of management competence in Britain is higher than it was before the recent crises. Sweeping changes in countless boardrooms have removed much of the dead wood. Both strategic thinking and operational control have improved enormously.

The competitive pressures of the last decade have forced managers to be much clearer about their objectives and the values that underlie them. They are conscious that they are competing internationally. Most of them also realize that they are shooting at a moving target — a target whose rate of improvement has, historically, exceeded their own.

This has, in many cases, led to a search for 'worldwide best practice' and an effort to match it in the UK. Schweppes were dedicated exponents of this 'benchmark' technique. They were also good, incidentally, at concentrating orders for a particular product line into just one factory, loading it to capacity in order to see what efficiencies can be obtained when it is running at its absolute maximum or slightly beyond.

Having one's objectives clear also makes it easier to produce a mission statement, providing a focus for effort. Burton defined their mission as being 'the retail fashion leaders of the eighties'. This gave impetus to their divestment of Rymans and other acquisitions that added nothing to their central purpose. It also helped to clarify their segmentation of the market and the realignment of their stores.

Overall mission statements, suitable for an entire organization, need refining for individual divisions and departments. The values which underlie the mission statement will be interpreted differently according to circumstances. For example, the maintenance division of a small but rapidly growing computer company defined its mission as 'protecting the quality image of the company and keeping it in business'. This was compatible with the company's overall mission of providing high-quality products incorporating leading-edge technology. It also, however, focussed on the role of the maintenance department in protecting against the adverse consequences for quality of too-hasty design and rapid new-model introduction.

The mission statement, as well as being tailored to each sub-unit, needs to be backed-up by a clear formulation of goals. These should be quantified and time-constrained so that they provide a real yardstick for performance. Like all good goals, they should also achieve that delicate balance of being challenging but feasible.

Greater clarity in mission and goals also makes it easier to decentralize decision-making. Competitive pressures, cost-cutting and demanning have made decentralization an important objective of most successful companies. This is difficult to achieve if goals are unclear.

Decentralization has meant a reduction in levels of management, with a consequent flattening of the hierarchy. The reduction in levels of management has been quite dramatic. For example, Rothmans talk of a reduction from as high as nine levels down to three, and Pilkington from seven to three. Decentralization and flattening of hierarchies have several consequences. First, it means that more local accountability is expected. The centre has to be prepared to grant local management the authority necessary to discharge its new responsibilities. Provided the financial control systems are well designed and properly implemented, this should be no problem.

Good financial controls are also important since a broadening of the span of control, as the hierarchy is flattened, means there will be less time available for reviewing the decisions of decentralized management. This, in turn, has the beneficial effect that the limited time available is more likely to be concentrated on the key decisions that relate to strategy and fundamental product/market issues.

Shorter lines of communication put managers at senior levels in closer touch with the action on the shopfloor. Local accountability means there is less room for staff IR functions to intervene between the managers and the workforce. Managers can talk directly with the people they manage and have an opportunity to convey to them their vision and values. They can generate the team spirit that comes from being together in the survival ark.

This strengthening of direct contact with the workforce, allowing neither unions nor IR departments to intervene, can be seen as a reassertion of management authority. In a way, it is — but not in the old authoritarian sense. Managers nowadays want to make their case direct to the workforce and influence them to help achieve the strategic objectives. The more successful of them will do their utmost to explain the objectives clearly. They will be completely open in providing the necessary background information to make the objectives clear and acceptable. Above all, they will remain sensitive to feedback from the workforce that may provide strategic insight and help them improve.

More important, however, managers want direct contact with the workforce so that their energies can be released by the creation of commitment. There are ideas and talents in abundance to be tapped. Managers are increasingly aware of this and less inclined to stifle it by pursuing the old authoritarian line. As Pat Lowry, chairman of ACAS, has put it, 'A readiness to communicate and consult has to be based on far longer-term considerations than putting the fear of God into employees in time of recession'. Employee involvement, he adds, is not just a 'thunderstorm' practice, to be switched on and off at will; it is needed in all kinds of economic weather.

In a sense, the better managers have become dedicated to achieving success; willing to give up status symbols and autocratic ways in order to bridge the gap between 'them and us', so that everyone can pull together in the survival ark.

Index